condemned to repeat it

condemned

▼

THE PHILOSOPHER WHO FLUNKED LIFE AND

▼

VIKING

to repeat it

OTHER GREAT LESSONS FROM HISTORY ▲

Wick Allison,
Jeremy Adams,
► and Gavin Hambly

VIKING
Published by the Penguin Group
Penguin Putnam Inc., 375 Hudson Street,
New York, New York 10014, U.S.A.
Penguin Books Ltd, 27 Wrights Lane, London W8 5TZ, England
Penguin Books Australia Ltd, Ringwood, Victoria, Australia
Penguin Books Canada Ltd, 10 Alcorn Avenue, Toronto, Ontario, Canada M4V 3B2
Penguin Books (N.Z.) Ltd, 182–190 Wairau Road, Auckland 10, New Zealand

Penguin Books Ltd, Registered Offices:
Harmondsworth, Middlesex, England

First published in 1998 by Viking Penguin, a member of Penguin Putnam Inc.

10 9 8 7 6 5 4 3 2 1

Grateful acknowledgment is made for permission to reprint excerpts from the following copyrighted works:
   The Nobility of Failure: Tragic Stories in the History of Japan by Ivan Morris. © 1975 by Ivan Morris. Reprinted by permission of Henry Holt and Company, Inc.
   The Little Flowers of Saint Francis, translated by Leo Sherley-Price (Penguin Classics, 1959). Copyright © Leo Sherley-Price, 1959. Reprinted by permission of Penguin Books Ltd.
   "The Lanercost Chronicle" from *Life in the Middle Ages* edited and translated by G. G. Coulton. By permission of Cambridge University Press.

LIBRARY OF CONGRESS CATALOGING IN PUBLICATION DATA
Allison, Wick.
   Condemned to repeat it : the philosopher who flunked life and other great lessons from history / Wick Allison, Jeremy Adams, and Gavin Hambly.
      p.   cm.
   Includes bibliographical references.
   ISBN 0-670-85951-6
   1. History—Miscellanea.   2. Leadership.   I. Adams, Jeremy.   II. Hambly, Gavin. date.
   III. Title.
D10.A57   1998
909—dc21   98-5536

This book is printed on acid-free paper.
∞

Printed in the United States of America
Set in Minion
Designed by Ellen Cipriano

To our children and grandchildren

We have the need of history, not to fall back on,
but to see if we can escape from it.

ORTEGA Y GASSET

Acknowledgments

Jeremy Adams and Gavin Hambly, both professors with a rollicking good sense of history's pleasures and mysteries, agreed with the idea behind this book and pitched in to make it happen. "Anybody can have an idea," an editor of mine once posted as a sign on her desk, and by that she meant that she had heard enough bright ideas and was still waiting for most of them to see the light of day. Jeremy and Gavin brought this idea to life, and I will always be grateful for the erudition, hard work, and good spirit with which they tackled the task.

John Boswell listened to my first rough thoughts, grasped immediately what I was after, gave the project shape and direction, and recommended it to Viking, where Mindy Werner took charge and made it into a book. Those who say there are no great editors left in book publishing have never had the pleasure of working with Mindy, whose patience is exceeded only by her good judgment.

Sara Peterson organized the mountains of material we produced, winnowed through it, researched most of it, disproved some of it, and skillfully and diplomatically shepherded the work to completion. She made all things possible.

I would also like to thank David Bauer, Al Allison, and John Peterson for their careful reading of various drafts and their many excellent editorial suggestions.

Special thanks to my wife, Christine, simply the most remarkable person I have ever met.

An undertaking such as this requires many hands, but only one can hold the helm. Any errors, omissions, and oversights are mine alone.

—W.A.

Contents

Introduction

"Those who cannot remember the past," wrote George Santayana, "are condemned to repeat it."

All of us know the quote. Most of us probably agree with it. But very few of us can recall the specific lessons of the past we're supposed to remember.

First of all, history is too grand and sweeping a panorama. Its movements arise in waves and wash over centuries, and its themes are too impossibly broad to apply to our everyday lives. As we all know, Rome was weakened from within by luxury and self-indulgence. The arrogance and brutality of the French aristocracy caused a revolution and cost them their lives. The Protestant ethic imbued America with a sense of manifest destiny that allowed it to conquer a continent and build an industrial superpower. But what can we learn from this knowledge that can actually help us?

Actually, quite a lot. Because behind the great themes are great men and women, the leaders of history. History by definition is about human beings, and there is nothing more fascinating, or more immediately applicable to our lives, than the study of human nature. History is a record of mankind's stupidities, pride, vindictiveness, hypocrisies, and ambitions, tempered by moments of heroism, grace, good judgment, and nobility. In the broad brush strokes of great themes these are sometimes hidden or obscured. But it is history's little stories that provide the greatest insight into the nature of man. Some are not pretty, some are powerful, and some are poignant. But the best of them are worth remembering precisely because they have something to teach.

These lessons are as applicable today as they ever were. After all, one doesn't need to be a contemporary of Cicero to discover that "some remedies are worse than the disease" (Publilius Syrus). Or an eighteenth-century prime minister of England to think "all men have their price" (Sir Robert Walpole). Or a nineteenth-century American poet to figure out that "there is no good arguing with the inevitable" (James Russell Lowell). Those lessons could apply tomorrow to decisions about personnel problems, a local school board vote, or a racquetball game.

Leaders particularly need the specific guidance that history can give them. "The only thing new in the world is the history you don't know," said Harry Truman. Caught up in the pressures and needs of the moment, we often forget that most questions have already been answered, and those answers are readily available to us if only we know where to look. Our sources are the stories in which men and women face situations analogous to our own.

We have organized this book to identify the major challenges that leaders face, and bring to light some stories from the past that address those challenges. Each story is followed by its lesson. We tried to provide a representation from all periods of history and from all points of the globe. But in attempting to achieve two such seemingly simple objectives we uncovered tidbits too enticing to pass over—several stories from a particular era, for example, that illustrated lessons too important to ignore. So the reader will encounter here three narratives from the Napoleonic period and two about the very real problems of accession to the throne in King David's day. They happened to make their points better than any others.

As Santayana intimated, most people are condemned to an

endless cycle of repeating mistakes others have already made or learned to avoid. Cicero said it a bit differently when he wrote that "to be ignorant of what happened before you were born is to remain forever a child." In this sense, those of us who look to history are always students.

We need to keep learning because history keeps being made. Every day modern twists are added to ancient lessons. That's what makes it so urgent that we learn as much as we can from the stories of those who came before. Because we are not only history's children, we are also its parents.

Wick Allison
Craigie Claire, New York

part one

FORGING STRATEGIES THAT WORK

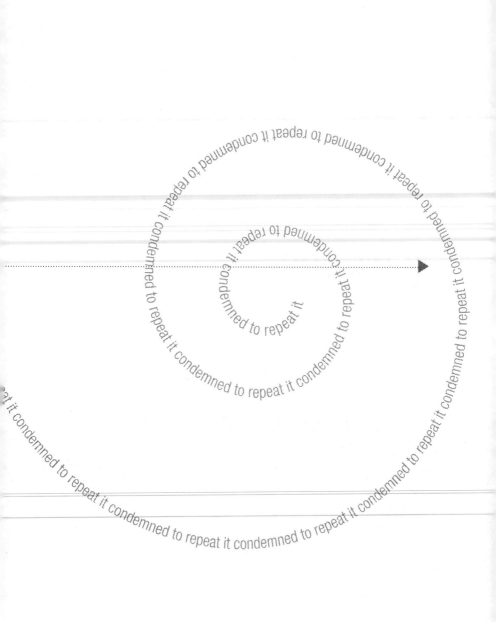
condemned to repeat it condemned to repeat it condemned to repeat it condemned to repeat it condemned to repeat it condemned to repeat it condemned to repeat it condemned to repeat it condemned to repeat it condemned to repeat it condemned to repeat it

The Roman Who Stared Down the Tyrant

Know when to bluff

A popular handbook on how to play *scopa,* an Italian card game, begins: "Rule Number One: always try to see your opponent's cards."

The corollary to this famous piece of advice is obvious: never let your opponent see your cards. Only then can a bluff work. That's the first rule, and to that add a second: a bluff only works if the other party believes you hold the cards.

And to that add a third rule: your opponent will only believe that you hold the cards if he thinks you never bluff.

In 149 B.C. the emperor Ssu-ma led his army to attack the stronghold of the warlord Chu-ko Liang, well known for the ferocity of his forces. As the imperial troops took up position for their attack, Chu-ko Liang suddenly struck his colors, stopped the beating of the drums, and threw open the gates to the city, revealing only a few men sweeping the grounds and tending the gardens. The emperor paused, suspecting an ambush. After some hesitation, Ssu-ma not only backed off from the seige, but withdrew entirely, fearing that Chu-ko's main force was about to surround him. This was exactly what the warlord had hoped for. An epidemic had ravaged his army, and he didn't have the strength to hold the city against an imperial attack.

Of course, sometimes the other side isn't bluffing. The Naval Institute magazine *Proceedings* reported this interchange: some years ago a lookout on a battleship spotted a light holding steady dead-ahead. The captain immediately ordered a signal to be sent, "Change your course." Back flashed the signal, "Change *your* course." The captain ordered a new signal, "I'm a captain. This is a battleship. I am proceeding ahead. Advise you change your course." Back came the signal, "I'm a seaman second-class. This is a lighthouse. Do what you want."

Bluffing requires a certain amount of gamesmanship, which the ancient Romans of the Republic were never known for. They were, in fact, known to be deadly serious about everything. "When a Roman smiles," sighed one Greek ambassador, "the world will crumble."

Rome in the second century B.C. watched warily over the uneasy balance of power between Egypt and Syria. Having destroyed Carthage years before, Rome was not about to allow another dominant power to ascend along the coasts of the Mediterranean, which the Romans referred to as *mare nostrum* ("our sea").

But by 168 B.C. a succession of dynastic quarrels among Egypt's royal family had so weakened the country internally that the Syrian monarch Antiochus Epiphanes decided to seize the moment. With an army of thirty thousand he quickly overran Egypt's frontier defenses, seized several important cities, and began a march on Alexandria, where the royal family had fled for protection. The Egyptians appealed to Rome for an army to repulse the invader.

In Rome, news of the disaster brought consternation to the Senate. Rome was in no position to take on a new enemy: its treasury and armies were depleted by the Punic Wars to the south and constant skirmishes with barbarians to the north. But, the Senate reasoned, nobody knew that—least of all a Syrian monarch a thousand miles away. So it dispatched one of its most prestigious members, the ex-consul Gaius Popillius Laenas, accompanied only by twelve lictors bearing the fasces, or bundles of sticks, that for centuries had symbolized Roman power.

Arriving in Alexandria in the fastest boat available, Laenas didn't bother to make a ceremonial appearance before the anxiously waiting royal court, but immediately walked out of the city and headed east, in the direction of the invading Syrian army. Laenas was an old man, and he walked slowly but deliberately, relying on a tall staff to help him, and after several hours he and his lictors encountered the outriders of Antiochus' army.

Shocked at the appearance of a lone Roman senator on the road in front of them, the advance guard and soon the entire army behind it came to an abrupt halt. Within minutes Antiochus and his entourage came riding up from the rear to investigate the delay. Seeing the senator standing in the middle of the road, the king dismounted and angrily strode up to him.

"What are you doing in Egypt?" he demanded.

"Your Majesty, I believe the question rather is, What are *you* doing in Egypt?" replied the aged senator.

The king laughed. "Go back to Rome, old man," he said.

The senator didn't move. The king stopped laughing.

"Who do you think you are?" he demanded. "Behind me stands an army of thirty thousand men."

The senator seemed unimpressed. "Behind you stands only a visible and rather small army. Behind me stand the invisible legions of Rome. In the name of the Senate and People of Rome, I order you to go home."

The king glared at the senator and, trembling with anger, seemed about to reach for his sword. As he hesitated, Gaius Popillius Laenas quietly stepped forward and with the end of his staff drew a circle in the dirt around the Syrian monarch. When he had returned to his position he looked Antiochus in the face.

"Step out of the circle, King, in any direction but east, and you will answer with your kingdom and your life."

The king stood transfixed, staring at the old man in the dusty toga blocking his way. Even through the dirt he could not have failed to see the toga's purple border, nor did he have to be told what those bundles of sticks represented. The king studied the senator. The old man did not move. The sun beat down on the thousands of troops and snorting animals. The senator waited impassively, not so much as shifting his weight, his eyes never moving in their solemn gaze. Behind the king the captains of his army waited in growing amazement. Time passed. The sun grew hotter.

Suddenly the king did an about-face and stepped out of the circle, heading east. Without a word he remounted his horse and wheeled it back toward the rear of his army as his captains shouted orders to reverse course.

Gaius Popillius Laenas stood for a while longer alone in the middle of the road, then signaled his lictors to begin the long walk back to Alexandria. In the old Roman way, he didn't crack a smile.

▶ Remember: A bluff works only when it is believed, and you will be believed only if you are known not to bluff. Play your cards carefully, and never show your hand to anyone.

Why MacArthur Turned a Cartwheel

Go around obstacles to get at the objective

Obstacles are a fact of life. Nobody's path to success is straight, open, and rose-strewn. More likely it will be uphill, rock-laden, and overgrown with thorn bushes. Obstacles of one sort or another will present themselves at every turn. How we deal with them is a matter of character. But it's also a matter of strategy.

When faced with an obstacle many people will hit it head-on. They lose sight of their original objective and concentrate everything on the obstacle that prevents them from achieving it. Mistaking the obstacle for the objective, they smash up against it.

In war the objective is clearly to win. The only way to win is to kill more of the enemy's side than the enemy kills of your side. (When this truism of military logic became evident to the ancient Chinese, they came up with an elegant solution. Before a battle the generals frequently would count the number of soldiers, then agree that whichever side had mustered the larger army had won the day.)

In war, overcoming an obstacle can cost dearly. Even the smallest force can inflict immense damage and cause delay. Stranded far from home, Charles XII of Sweden with only forty men once held off for eight hours the ten thousand Turks sent to surprise and capture him. The 189 Texans at the Alamo held off five thousand Mexicans for nearly two weeks. At the narrow pass of Thermopylae fourteen hundred Greeks under Leonidas kept an entire Persian invasion at bay until they were betrayed—even so, they died fighting to the last man.

These are the kinds of obstacles no general wants to encounter. But in the battle for the Pacific during World War II, Douglas MacArthur faced one even worse. Pearl Harbor had been but one phase of a huge two-pronged Japanese offensive that swept down the central and eastern Pacific. If the Allies had any hope of breaking out from their defensive position and turning the offensive tide against the Japanese, they would first have to confront the entrenched Japanese position at Rabaul.

For their part, the Japanese threatened to invade Australia. After the Battle of Midway in June 1942 had checked their advance in the central Pacific, the Japanese continued almost unimpeded southward through the Solomon Islands and overland down into New Guinea. MacArthur, who had been holed up in threatened Australia after the loss of the Philippines, was given orders that reflected more hope than expectation: halt the enemy advance, drive them out of the Solomons and New Guinea, and, most of all, eliminate the great base the enemy had established at Rabaul, on the island of New Britain in the Bismarck Archipelago. Rabaul was a perfect launching pad for the Japanese invasion of Australia, with a spacious natural harbor that held one of the largest concentrations of Japanese warships in the Pacific. As a prelude to the conquest of the South Pacific, the small island had been garrisoned with a hundred thousand troops and supplied with hundreds of aircraft.

For his part, MacArthur first needed a beachhead, and at Guadalcanal on the southern tip of the Solomons (which themselves almost touch Australia) he fought to establish one. The fierceness of the Japanese counterattack and the courage of the enemy defenders led MacArthur to reconsider the orders he had been given. In effect, he decided that an assault on Rabaul would be suicidal.

MacArthur decided to go around it.

His plan to go around Rabaul was called Operation Cartwheel, and it began in September 1943. First, his air forces attacked and destroyed the enemy's aircraft and landing fields at Rabaul. That gave him cover to move northward around the island. Next, he landed troops on two small island groups above Rabaul. That made enemy reinforcement impossible. As MacArthur continued his drive north, he left the hundred thousand Japanese at Rabaul isolated and, by mid-1944, starving to death.

The brilliance of MacArthur's strategy shows in the numbers. In the entire Pacific campaign the Americans lost fewer than fifty thousand men.

Contrast that with just one battle in the European theater. At about the same time Rabaul was being encircled and ignored, the U.S. Fifth Army, bogged down in its invasion of Italy from the south, decided to try to break the Germans' Gustav Line by directly assaulting Anzio, a little town on the sea south of Rome. General Mark Clark made a seaborne assault that went up against the strength of the German army. In one four-month, head-on clash on one beach, Clark lost twenty-eight thousand men— about half the number of men that MacArthur lost in the four years of his entire campaign.

MacArthur was a student of military history, and even at one point superintendent of West Point. No doubt he had studied one of the first handbooks ever written on military strategy, Julius Caesar's *Gallic Wars*.

In his book (a sensation in Rome when it was published; no

general before had been as literary-minded or publicity-driven to think of such a thing), Caesar relates the moment of his gravest danger in the long struggle to subdue Gaul. While wintering in northern Italy in 52 B.C. Caesar received word that Vercingetorix, the most capable of the Gallic chiefs, had united nearly all the Gallic tribes in rebellion. Caesar's predicament was that his army was cut in two: one half was with him, and the other half was in the north of Gaul. Vercingetorix occupied the middle. Coming from the south, Caesar encountered the Gallic army in a strong defensive position waiting for his attack. Not wanting to waste his legions in a battle where the outcome was uncertain, Caesar did the unthinkable for a Roman general in front of an enemy. He ignored it. He simply went around it. Leaving troops to lull Vercingetorix into thinking he had the Romans in sight, Caesar made one of those lightning moves for which he became famous and reunited with his main army in the north.

Vercingetorix must have still been pondering over that move months later as he was led in chains in Caesar's triumphal march through the streets of Rome. Two thousand years later, MacArthur probably pondered it as well while he walked along the beaches of Guadalcanal and wondered how to win his war.

▶ Remember: Your opponent knows what he is doing. But he doesn't know what you'll do. When he throws up an obstacle that is insurmountable, you can attack it—or like MacArthur you can ignore it, leaving him with the cost and you with the momentum.

The Forty-seven *Ronin*

Strike a balance between competing objectives

Sometime after World War II the author Luigi Barzini found himself in a ludicrous position. A friend had been so deeply insulted by a column in a Communist newspaper that the man felt he had no recourse but to challenge the offending journalist to a duel. Barzini and his friend pored over an old copy of Jacopo Gelli's *Italian Code of Chivalry*, which gives the rules for resolving disputes among gentlemen (then wasted several hours arguing over whether a Communist could be a gentleman). Following the procedures of the book Barzini then asked to meet the journalist in a crowded café, and amid the bustling waiters and laughing patrons, handed the man the formal letter as prescribed by Gelli's rules. The smiling journalist's face quickly paled, and he became very grave. This was a serious matter, he said, and therefore he must first refer it to the party. After much debate within the party's highest councils (these were, after all, *Italian* Communists) the duel was forbidden. Barzini later wrote that he remained grateful to the Communist party forever after. Two objectives had been accomplished. Honor had been preserved, and nobody had been shot.

Questions of honor are always perplexing, and usually dangerous. That's why they can be instructive lessons in how to achieve competing ends.

In eighteenth-century Japan the government's major problem was the code of Bushido—the Way of the Warrior—a set of moral precepts that extolled the medieval virtues of the warrior caste. Loyalty, personal honor, reverence for the past, and obedience to one's superiors were all embedded in the code.

This military ethic was fine in times of war. The problem was that Japan had long been at peace. But the aristocracy and its samurai retainers were imbued with a warrior mentality, causing the authorities no end of trouble. The slightest offense would cause brawls, duels, and vendettas. Masterless samurai—known as *ronin* (literally, "waves")—roamed the countryside, extremely conscious of their caste, highly trained in the fighting arts, but unemployed and looking to prove their mettle.

The quandary was that the aristocratic government believed in Bushido. But it also recognized the need to establish a rule of law if the government was to have any control whatsoever. How to compel obedience to the law, when Bushido made every samurai a law unto himself?

The great matter came to a head over a small insult.

In 1700 a noble of the middle rank named Asano was rehearsing the etiquette of a state ceremony at the shogun's palace in Yedo. To be called to Yedo to participate in such an occasion was a matter of great prestige. While teaching Asano the intricate maneuvers required of him in the ceremony, his instructor, a high-ranking shogunate official named Kira, made a disparaging remark about his pupil. Asano whipped out his sword and slashed Kira. He was immediately arrested, and his punishment was never in doubt. To raise a weapon in the palace was bad enough, but to wound a representative of the shogun was fatal. Asano was sent home in disgrace and ordered to commit suicide.

Asano's personal cadre of forty-seven samurai were now masterless. They were *ronin*. They were also aggrieved. Asano had behaved honorably. He had responded to an insult to his name. And when ordered to kill himself, he had done so without hesitation or complaint. But what about Kira—and what about the insult?

The forty-seven *ronin* scattered, some to their former homes, others to distant towns and villages. They knew Kira would be on guard, and that his men would be trying to trace their whereabouts. For two years they each managed to escape detection; meanwhile, when it seemed clear they had all fled for their lives and would be heard from no more, Kira and his entourage relaxed.

On a snowy night in February 1703, by prearranged plan, the forty-seven *ronin* converged at a spot outside the city gates of Yedo. In groups of two and three, they managed to slip past the shogun's guards at various checkpoints. Reassembling in the darkened street outside Kira's mansion, they attacked just before dawn. Kira was slaughtered before the alarm could be raised. As the sun rose, the avenged *ronin* lined up in front of the mansion, each man's right arm red with Kira's blood, each equal in his guilt, ready to be arrested and executed for the crime.

For a year the government—and the nation—debated over what to do with these assassins.

Strict Confucians argued that they should be set free, and the shogun himself was disposed in their favor. After all, they had properly avenged the insult to their master, and in doing so they had displayed an honor and loyalty that should be extolled.

Political philosophers argued that while loyalty is a fine attribute, how it is brought to action must be considered within the limits of the law. If these *ronin* were set free, all Japan would be set loose to interpret loyalty however it wanted. Perhaps they might even reinterpret their loyalty to the shogun.

As the government discussions went this way and that, popular sentiment for the *ronin* built to a fever pitch. If the shogun now executed the murderers, the backlash would be immense. Finally the government hit upon a solution.

For an act of honor these men must pay a debt of honor. The *ronin* were offered a high compliment: they were invited to commit hara-kiri, an honor hitherto only available to the nobility. All forty-seven accepted. With their voluntary deaths, Bushido paid deference to the law; the warrior code submitted itself to the civil code. The balance established by their examples would be enough to steady Japan until its eventual emergence into the modern world.

▶ Remember: Competing ends need not cancel each other out. Nor do they have to be mutually exclusive. You may be able to find a balance that achieves both goals. But don't go back and forth between the two. Choose a path that accomplishes both.

The General Who Wouldn't Fight

Know when to do nothing

When encountering a rhinoceros the thing to do is to stand perfectly still. The animal is partially blind; movement only attracts his attention. As a good test of your self-control, try standing still while a one-ton killer ambles along in front of you. If that's not a problem, you're probably the type of person who sticks an angry letter in a desk drawer for twenty-four hours before deciding whether to send it. Knowing when to do nothing is a rare talent, and very few people possess it. One Russian had this talent to a remarkable degree, and Napoleon Bonaparte never recovered from it.

In October of 1812, just as the brutal Russian winter was about to set in, Napoleon ordered the French army to abandon burned-out Moscow and to begin one of the most inglorious and famous retreats in history. Within weeks the most victorious army that had ever marched was reduced to a pathetic mob: devastated by disease, frozen and hungry, ragged and virtually unarmed, every day dying by the scores along the rutted and muddy roads.

From a distance the disintegration of Napoleon's *grande armee* was watched by an obese old man resting on a swaybacked bay horse. Field Marshal Mikhail Illarionovich Kutuzov had lost one eye in a battle years before and his remaining one was embedded in folds of fat. His tunic buttons popped open so often he quit replacing them, so that the undershirt over his belly was the most regular and visible part of his uniform. He wore only the white cap of a common horse-guard, with no peak or insignia, and indeed the only sign that this was the commander in chief of All Russia was the squadron of immaculately dressed, colorfully feathered, and heavily medaled officers on horseback who surrounded him at a deferential remove.

Every now and then one of those officers would summon the courage to spur his horse forward, and once close enough would bend over to whisper a suggestion in the old man's good right ear:

cut the retreat in two and capture half the force; raid the supply trains and destroy the few remaining provisions; set up artillery downcountry and rake the forward line. After every suggestion the face resting with repose on that capacious double chin would nod solemnly, whether in sympathy with the request or in rhythm with his breathing one could not tell, and the right hand would lazily wave the intruder back to his place.

Field Marshal Kutuzov would end this war the way he had won it: by doing nothing.

Only with evident distaste and embarrassment had Tsar Alexander I summoned Kutuzov to the supreme post, despite his enviable string of victories throughout a fifty-year career of service. Unlike the Prussian generals the tsar had imported into his army, with their parade-ground precision and stiff military bearing, Kutuzov was a Russian of the old school, which in the tsar's eyes meant that for all his noble pedigree he was little better than a peasant. But as Napoleon proceeded to rout the Prussian commanders in every encounter, the nation clamored for a patriot to lead its army. The tsar finally relented and put the ungainly old war hero in charge, saying to an aide, "The public wanted Kutuzov; I appointed him. As for me, I wash my hands of it."

Kutuzov, for his part, knew two things: that the public wanted a general who would fight, which everyone knew, and that a fight was no way to beat Napoleon, which nobody else seemed to know.

He decided for morale's sake to give the public what it wanted, if only to secure his own position, and he met Napoleon at Borodino outside Moscow, where his ill-equipped and badly organized army was soundly defeated. The panic in Russia grew wilder, but Kutuzov merely moved his remaining troops out of the French emperor's way, saying placidly: "Napoleon is like a torrent that cannot be stopped. Moscow is like a sponge that absorbs the flood." From that day forward Kutuzov never allowed another full-scale engagement.

While the tsar fumed, while his generals petitioned, while messengers flew back and forth between army divisions and the court at St. Petersburg, Kutuzov spent his time writing elegant letters to Madame de Staël, reading his favorite French novelists, and cavorting with his mistress. At staff meetings his generals pored over maps, planned battles, and argued over tactics, only to be interrupted midstream by the sound of snoring from the end of the table where sat their commander in chief. When a field commander came to report, "he was obviously hearing it simply because he had ears," wrote Count Leo Tolstoy, "but it was obvious that nothing that general could possibly say could surprise or interest him, that he knew beforehand all that he would be told, and listened only because he had to . . . What the general was saying was practical and sensible, but apparently Kutuzov despised both knowledge and intellect, and knew of something else that would settle things—something different, quite apart from intellect and knowledge." Kutuzov knew he had no army to match the French, no generals capable of outmaneuvering the famed imperial marshals, and no time to train or develop either. To give Napoleon a fight would be to give him Russia.

The French were baffled. They attempted stratagem after stratagem to lure the old man into battle. They tried to stir up revolt against the tsar. They feinted toward St. Petersburg. They sent probes deep into Kutuzov's flanks. Alexander himself was apoplectic, the court was panic-stricken, the general staff was enraged—and meanwhile Kutuzov was asleep. Outside the snow began to fall. The Russian winter had begun.

The old marshal died in April of 1813 in Prussia, where he was still following at a distance the bedraggled and decimated French army as it stumbled its way home. A year later Napoleon was forced into exile. He was to make a last effort at a comeback in 1815, but his forces were too spent to withstand the combined allied powers.

They had never recovered from their long encounter with the Russian general who wouldn't fight.

▶ **Remember: If Kutuzov had committed his inferior army against Napoleon, he would have lost. Even when attacked, you don't necessarily have to fight. You do have to know when to act—and when to let nature take its course.**

The Proconsul Who Longed for His Laurels

Set clear steps to reach any goal

The Bay of Pigs fiasco in 1961 was a classic case of when goals are confused with strategy. President John Kennedy agreed to a plan for the invasion of Cuba, then made a stipulation: to avoid international censure, no American forces would participate. The stipulation was mere fig leaf, since the whole world knew the United States was the sponsor. But Kennedy's last-minute requirement changed everything. Without naval and air support, no invasion can succeed, as World War II veterans in the Pentagon should have known. The invasion went ahead anyway. Every man on the beaches was either killed or captured.

Goals are easy to state. In that case, the goal was to overthrow Castro. But without a clearly defined strategy a goal means nothing. "Our goal is to make money," a business owner tells his staff. He thinks he has stated a goal, but in effect he has said nothing. "Our goal is to deliver ninety percent of our product to ninety percent of our customers on time," is Peter Drucker's favorite example. This statement has the benefit of sounding precise while being absolutely meaningless. (Unless the hidden message is that ten percent of the company's customers are never supposed to receive any product at all.)

For every goal there must be a strategy. "My goal is to become the most envied woman in France," the lovely eighteen-year-old Marie de Rabutin-Chantal told the handsome Henri de Sévigné in 1644. "And how do you plan to accomplish that?" asked the amused marquis. "By marrying you," replied Marie. And she did.

When a goal is set without a clear strategy to accomplish it the results can be even more disastrous than the Bay of Pigs was in American history, as the single worst defeat in the annals of Rome shows.

The Roman senator Marcus Licinius Crassus had grown so rich and powerful by 60 B.C. he was able to elbow himself into the First Triumvirate with Pompey and Caesar. But Crassus lacked the one thing that brought real honor in Rome. He had not led an army to victory over one of Rome's enemies. Pompey had defeated Mithradates, bringing the East into Rome's hegemony, and also had cleared the Mediterranean of pirates. Caesar had been awarded the civic crown for his valor as a young man, and was earning more laurels by bringing Gaul under Roman domination.

Crassus' failure to achieve anything comparable grated on him, and even though he was in his sixties, he was determined to redress it. He demanded that Pompey and Caesar agree to his taking the governorship of Syria. There, he dreamed, he would follow in the steps of Alexander the Great, conquer Parthia, and march on India. He would gain glory beyond the dreams of Pompey and Caesar.

In the spring of 54 B.C. he arrived in Syria and provisioned an army of seven legions, more than forty thousand men. He had little cavalry but he expected the king of Armenia to provide a mounted force. As he planned his invasion, his captains advised against crossing the Euphrates and plunging straight into Parthian territory. Better, they counseled, to cross the mountainous regions of Armenia, where the infantry would have an advantage over the famed Parthian horsemen. But Crassus was intent on taking Seleucia, the great metropolis on the Tigris, and he could not be dissuaded.

A Parthian envoy appeared at the Roman camp and was brought before Crassus. The envoy, knowing Crassus' reputation in Rome, asked if these preparations signified a war with Rome or merely a private little war for Crassus' personal enrichment. Nettled, Crassus said he would answer in Seleucia. Extending the palm of his hand, the envoy laughed and quipped, "Hair will grow here before you see Seleucia."

The Armenian king arrived, bringing with him an escort of only six thousand riders, not the forty thousand troops he had promised. He, too, tried to convince Crassus to advance through the mountains. When the Roman rejected his advice, he abruptly decamped and returned home. The aristocratic Cassius, quaestor of the army, urged that without sufficient cavalry the expedition should be abandoned, but Crassus was intent on winning his laurels.

The army crossed the Euphrates in a violent storm, which did nothing to improve the morale of the troops. Morale sank lower, even among the most seasoned veterans, when they were fed lentils and salt, the traditional food for funerals. Then Crassus, who had never led troops before, announced he was destroying the bridge they had just crossed, "so that none of you may return." Even if he was aware of the alarm this announcement caused, he was too obstinate to correct it.

At first the army marched close to the river, but soon scouts returned from the desert, where they reported signs of many horses' hooves. Crassus interpreted this to mean the Parthians had approached and fled at the sight of the superior Roman force. At this moment a Bedouin chief appeared, telling the Romans exactly what Crassus already thought. Crassus, a homeboy unused to the intrigues of the East, didn't suspect that the Bedouin had been paid to throw the Romans offtrack.

Eager to attack the enemy, Crassus set off with his army across the desert at double pace, forcing the infantry to keep up with his horsemen. Suddenly the scouts reported that the enemy was not fleeing, but approaching. The exhausted troops were now thrown into consternation, and to increase the confusion Crassus at first ordered a long front with the cavalry on the wings, then changed his mind and ordered the troops drawn up in a square.

The Parthians, for their part, began the attack with small numbers of poorly armed men. The thought of easy victory drew the Romans out of their ranks until suddenly they found themselves confronted by the main Parthian army, well armed and well equipped. The Romans quickly re-formed their ranks and repulsed the first onslaught. The Parthians then sent in their archers who—with their famous "Parthian shot"—poured a seeming cloudburst of arrows on the Romans.

Night brought an end to the engagement but not to the army's sufferings. Crassus tried a retreat, but the wounded left on the field sent up such a cry that the Parthians were alerted to the move. Crassus and some of his men made it to the nearby town of Carrhae, but the next morning they were caught and slain.

Crassus' defeat had cost Rome twenty thousand dead and ten

thousand taken captive. Surena, the enemy commander, paraded the heads of the dead in a long procession through the streets of Seleucia.

The disaster at Carrhae would be emblazoned in the minds of Romans for centuries to come, and Crassus would go down in their histories as one of the greatest fools the nation ever produced. As greedy for glory as he was for gold, he had handed Rome the worst defeat in its history.

▶ **Remember: If asked what his goal was, Crassus would have replied, "To beat the Parthians." But his real goal was to gain a triumph in Rome to upstage his rivals. Having confused his goal, he confused his strategy. He was so eager to meet the enemy—to achieve his real goal—that he played into its hands. Use this rule: if you can't clearly lay out the steps to achieve it, you don't have a goal. You only have a hope.**

The Lady Pirate Who Ruled the Sea

Negotiate from strength

After the Franco-Austrian battle of Solferino in 1859, in which both sides suffered huge casualties, Napoleon III sued for peace. A general objected, saying both sides were still evenly matched. "I don't like war," the emperor replied. "There's too much luck involved."

Peace is an art as much as war is, and knowing when and how to negotiate peace is the art's highest form. The most successful pirate of all time knew how to negotiate from strength.

Our most famous pirates—with names like Blackbeard, Henry Morgan, Calico Jack, and Black Bart—plied their trade, flying their Jolly Rogers, in the West Indies of the seventeenth and eighteenth centuries. But famous as these notorious buccaneers might be in Western lore, they were like boys playing in a sandbox compared to a young woman named Hsi Kai.

Hsi Kai was peacefully going about her business as a prostitute when she was plucked from a Cantonese brothel during a pirate raid in 1801. Captured as plunder by associates of the notorious Ching Yih, who operated freely along South China's coast, Hsi Kai and her fellow prisoners were brought before the pirate captain for his review. The twenty-six-year-old Hsi Kai had apparently enjoyed her profession, and resented the interruption, because when Ching Yih walked in front of her, thoughtfully calculating the value of his new assets, she plunged at him and nearly scratched his eyes out. The pirate chief was immediately infatuated with her, and after some serious negotiations Hsi Kai agreed to become his wife, but only after she had wrangled fifty percent ownership of his far-flung enterprises.

Ching Yih operated with six fleets—red, blue, yellow, green, black, and white. Within months Hsi Kai persuaded her husband to give her command of the white fleet, whether as a stratagem to get out of the house or from a genuine desire to learn the trade we will never know. By the time Ching Yih was killed in a typhoon in 1807, his wife had proved herself so successful as a commander that she was able to demand—and receive—the fealty of his captains. Now she was sole owner of the business, and soon she was well on her way to making it a monopoly on the South China seas.

Hsi Kai was something of an organizational genius. To provision her fleets and to keep from antagonizing the inland communities as her husband had done with his constant raids, she contracted with hundreds of farmers and merchants along the coast to supply food, clothing, and material. Villages that didn't agree to her terms were simply burned to the ground; the more compliant were visited with instant prosperity.

Within two years Hsi Kai was more powerful than most governments of the era. At a time when the United States Navy could probably put no more than fifty ships to sea, she commanded two hundred ocean-going ships, each carrying more than four hundred trained men and armed with twenty to thirty cannons. Along the coast she commanded eight hundred lighter ships, each heavily armed and carrying two hundred men. She had dozens of oared riverboats that plied up and down the inland waterways, enforcing her law. Trade between the ports of Hong Kong and Macao as well as along the Chinese coast was subject to her tax.

Hsi Kai's operations began to affect the wealth of nations. In 1810 the governments of Britain, Portugal, and China decided on a combined assault to protect legitimate trade. An attack was a calculated risk, since Hsi Kai's forces had outflanked or defeated every previous attempt to curtail them.

The emperor of China decided on one last entreaty, sending an emissary with this message, "If there is anything of a woman's heart in you, you will someday want peace and offspring. Could it be now?"

Hsi Kai was not one to be swayed by appeals to her femininity, but she was one to be alarmed by news of three great navies preparing to go to war against her.

On April 18, Hsi Kai suddenly appeared with a delegation of seventeen women at the residence of the governor-general in Canton and announced her willingness to negotiate. Fearing her arrest would result in massive retaliation, the governor agreed to deal with this woman as an equal. The government, after all, was eager for a settlement, well aware of the casualties and destruction that would be caused by an outright war.

Hsi Kai and the governor haggled all morning. With her usual skill, Hsi Kai won agreement that if she surrendered her ships and arms, she and her pirates could keep their plunder. Not only that, but any of her men who wanted could enlist in the army, and her new lover, Chang Pao, would be given the rank of lieutenant in the navy, with command of twenty ships. The deal was done by afternoon.

Two days later Hsi Kai surrendered, and with her no less than 17,318 men. If this was not one of the largest navies in the world, it was without a doubt the largest private business in existence. At the time Hsi Kai was thirty-five years old.

▶ Remember: The time to negotiate is when you're at your strongest and when it will cost your opponent less to pay you than it would to go against you. That's how Hsi Kai, prostitute turned pirate captain, became one of the richest women of her time.

The King Who Couldn't Decide

Choose a side and stick with it

"The lowest circle in hell," wrote Dante in *The Divine Comedy*, "is reserved for those who in time of moral crisis maintained their neutrality." Not just in times of moral crisis. From a strategic point of view, neutrality is almost always the worst option. Yet it's the option most of us choose. When two titans are locked in battle, the prudent course seems to be to stay out of it. But what looks like prudence to the noncombatant looks like temporizing to the two locked in battle. A competitor or an opponent can be respected, but nobody trusts a temporizer.

The exceptions prove the rule. Switzerland was able to stay neutral in World War II because its mountains made it impassable. Spain had been ravaged by its own civil war, which had ended the year Hitler invaded Poland; it basically had nothing left to contribute to either side. Sweden was surrounded by German conquests; it would have been more trouble to garrison than it was to leave alone. Other nations that tried to maintain neutrality in the great conflict—Norway, Denmark, Belgium, the Netherlands—were eaten alive.

Machiavelli underscores the dangers of neutrality in *The Prince*: "A prince is respected when he is either a true friend or a downright enemy, that is to say, when, without any reservation, he declares himself in favor of one party against the others; which course will always be more advantageous than standing neutral, because if two of your powerful neighbors come to blows . . . he who conquers does not want doubtful friends who will not aid him in the time of trial, and he who loses will not harbor you because you did not willingly, sword in hand, court his fate."

Never imagine, says Machiavelli, that you can choose perfectly safe courses. Expect in even ordinary affairs that when you seek to avoid one trouble you will invariably create another.

In the face of the whirlwind called Napoleon many princes chose to run for safety, hoping that the storm would pass. But some storms are so powerful no shelter can withstand them.

Frederick the Great had raised Prussia from a small German state on par with a Saxony and a Bavaria into one of the great powers of Europe. "He was the one man of his time," wrote one biographer, "who could outwit Voltaire and teach Napoleon." Indeed, Napoleon revered the Prussian king; he read his published letters by campfire and exhorted his generals to follow the Prussian's principles.

The great king's only flaw was that he could not choose his heirs. By the time of the Napoleonic Wars, his nephew's son occupied the throne of Prussia.

Frederick William II was a man of virtue but not of action. In 1803 Napoleon seized Hanover, a small German electorate which the larger Prussia had promised to protect. The Prussian generals clamored for war, but the king was unmoved. Better to feed a hungry beast than anger him, he reasoned. In 1805 Austria went to war and asked for Prussia's help; the king resisted. Who knew how this would end? Finally, in late 1805, the French went too far. They marched through Prussian territory as if it were their own. Frederick William sought a meeting with Tsar Alexander I of Russia at Potsdam; together they swore at the tomb of Frederick the Great to stand against Napoleon. Alexander marched with his army south to Austerlitz, where he and the Austrians were routed. By the time Frederick William had mobilized his army, the great battle was over, and his new allies were fleeing for their lives.

The king had acted too late. Now he hastened to make amends with Napoleon. He signed a treaty and a defensive pact with France, and agreed to close his ports to British goods. But that only led to more trouble: without thinking twice, England declared war on Prussia, and within weeks British ships had sealed up Prussian ports.

Frederick William now had serious problems. Not only had the English—whom he never meant to offend in the first place—destroyed his trade, but the beast he was trying to feed had a hunger that could never be satisfied. Napoleon formed the Confederation of the Rhine with smaller German states, effectively sealing up Prussia.

The survival of Frederick William's kingdom was now at stake. Even his beautiful wife had taken to wearing a regimental uniform and parading in front of the troops to stir Frederick William to action. He once again mobilized his army and ordered a breakthrough to Saxony. Joined by many Saxons, his forces numbered two hundred thousand men. Enraged at this breach of faith, Napoleon didn't hesitate. He rushed to the front, ordered the attack, and on the same day—October 14, 1806—annihilated the Prussian armies in two separate battles, at Jena and Auerstedt. Two weeks later Napoleon was in Berlin.

The French emperor graciously allowed Prussia to continue to exist. The cost was half its territory and most of its treasury. In one swoop Prussia lost 5,250,000 of its 9,750,000 population. War reparations to France in the years 1806 to 1808 amounted to the nation's entire revenue.

The only thing that can be said in Frederick William's defense is that he held what remained of his country together and bided his time. Nine years later his generals would distinguish themselves and redeem Prussia's honor at Waterloo. Perhaps by then Machiavelli had been translated into German.

▶ Remember: When two great opponents are locked in battle and appeal for your help, choose sides. Whichever side wins, you'll gain the respect of one and the gratitude of the other. Fail to choose, and both will disrespect or mistrust you.

part two

WINNING AGAINST THE COMPETITION

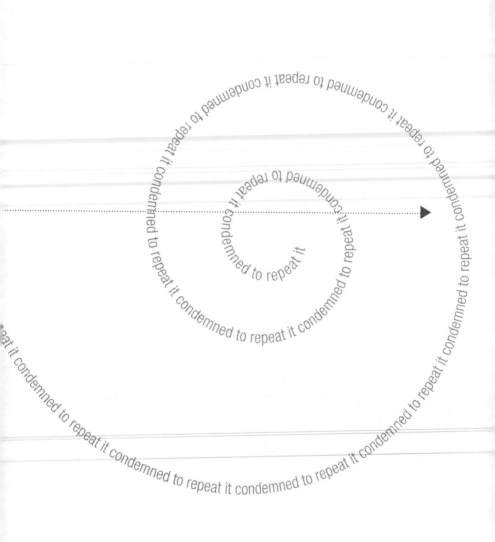

The Only Man Who Ever Beat Hannibal

Respect a talented opponent, and study his methods

Mechanical clocks first appeared in Europe in the fourteenth century, but the very first was constructed by a court official of the Sung dynasty in 1090. This "Heavenly Clockwork" was thirty feet high, built on five rising pagodas, with ninety-six jacks. Unfortunately for the Chinese, when a new emperor came to power in 1092 he viewed his predecessor's policies with contempt and, considering this new contraption symbolic of them, had it destroyed. When the Jesuit missionary Matteo Ricci arrived in China in 1583, he gained entry into the upper reaches of the usually xenophobic Chinese society largely because of an astonishing device he had brought with him: a mechanical clock.

Disdain for the achievements of others seems to be a characteristic of those who achieve power. The Portuguese introduced firearms and cannons to the Japanese in 1542. But when Tokugawa Ieyasu, who despised all things foreign, seized the shogunate in 1603, he outlawed these inferior inventions as unsuitable for true warriors. He confiscated them and forbade their manufacture. His prohibition of gunpowder was so strictly enforced that the memory of it had all but disappeared when Commodore Matthew Perry emphatically reminded the Japanese of its existence by firing his guns in Tokyo Bay in 1854.

Haughtiness is not uncommon even among those who are not emperors or shoguns, as the American automobile industry discovered to its own regret. Our opponents or competitors—or predecessors—have much to teach, but we are often so sure of our own superiority that we fail to learn.

There was no greater learner in history than Publius Cornelius Scipio, the Roman general charged with the mission of beating Carthage into submission. To accomplish this momentous task, Scipio would have to defeat the most brilliant strategist of his time, the Carthaginian general who had threatened Rome itself with his surprise crossing of the Alps, the great Hannibal Barca.

The thing about Scipio and Hannibal that intrigued their contemporaries is how alike they were. Both were raised from boyhood with the sole mission of destroying the other's country. Both were deeply shaped by their fathers, and both achieved glory beyond their fathers' dreams. On their fathers' deaths, both were appointed to assume their commands in Spain. Both seemed to believe they were reincarnations of Alexander the Great. Perhaps conscious of Alexander's foibles, both were ascetic in matters of sex, drink, and comfort. Both had a theatrical touch. Hannibal frequently dressed in costumes, constantly changing wigs, clothes, and walk (the hardest thing to disguise) to confuse potential assassins. Scipio would carefully study the tidal charts of bays when preparing to launch a seaborne assault, then at the right moment announce to his troops that Neptune himself was rising up to assist them.

But for all these similarities, there was one great difference. When Hannibal made his surprise crossing of the Alps in 218 B.C., losing half of his men and two thirds of his famous elephants, he was met at the rivers Ticinus and Trebia in northern Italy by two Roman armies under the command of Scipio's father. Even with his forces depleted and exhausted, Hannibal crushed the Roman defenders. The Roman commander himself was nearly killed, saved only at the last moment by his seventeen-year-old son, Scipio. From that day forward, the younger man would never underestimate the genius of Hannibal.

Sixteen years later the two were to meet again. Instead of trying to defeat Hannibal in Italy, which had proved fruitless, the Roman senate decided to send an invasion force to strike at Carthage itself. When the powerful army reached Sicily, Carthage sent a fleet to Italy to retrieve Hannibal so that he could prepare a defense.

In 202 B.C. the two great adversaries met at Zama, seventy-five miles southwest of Carthage. Under a flag of truce, Hannibal and Scipio tried to negotiate a peace settlement. The encounter fascinated all reporters. According to the Greek historian Polybius, Hannibal expressed regret that Carthage had ever sought territory outside Africa, and he suggested the same about Rome outside Italy. Hannibal proposed very simply that, since what was done was done, Carthage would withdraw to Africa, and that Rome could keep everything else. Scipio seems to have replied to the effect that a Carthage with a power base was a Carthage that could not be tolerated.

The following morning the two armies met on the field of battle to resolve the matter. The two were fairly well matched, with about thirty-five thousand men on each side. But Scipio had spent sixteen years studying Hannibal, and he was prepared for every tactical thrust and parry the practiced general could throw at him. By sunset it was clear the Roman legions had prevailed. The student had overcome the master.

Hannibal sued for peace, Carthage accepted Scipio's harsh terms, and Rome was now the undisputed power of the Mediterranean world. Scipio would thereafter be known as Scipio Africanus.

Scipio's respect for his great enemy became part of the lore of military history. Twenty-one centuries later two other great generals faced each other not far from where Scipio and Hannibal had clashed. The square-off between General George Patton and the German Erwin Rommel was to be decisive in the battle for North Africa, and Patton was ready for it. As he watched Rommel's tanks maneuver into a flanking position for their assault against the Allied forces, the general was heard to exclaim with satisfaction, "Rommel, you sonofabitch, I read your book!"

▶ Remember: Your competitor can be your greatest teacher. After all, he's the only one as interested in your business as you are. Watch his strategies, monitor his mistakes, and copy his successes.

How Solomon Became Known for Wisdom

Eliminate all rivals

To lose in a power struggle often means losing one's job. In rougher sports, like politics, it often means losing one's head. Stalin worked to consolidate his power after Lenin's death, and by 1930 he felt strong enough to exercise it: rivals Zinovyev, Kamenev, and Bukharin were condemned to death; Trotsky was assassinated. One year after becoming Germany's chancellor in 1933, Hitler brutally suppressed the SA, the feared storm troopers who had brought the Nazis to power; in the "Night of the Long Knives" SA chief Ernst Röhm and other leaders were murdered. Elimination of rivals is not a modern phenomenon. On having himself elected dictator in 82 B.C. Lucius Cornelius Sulla killed or exiled almost every other leader in Rome. Five hundred years before that, Cambyses II, on claiming the throne of his father, Cyrus the Great, put his brother to death along with several nobles—and even then he was following a well-established tradition.

Of course, these are four of history's notable madmen, and madmen have no conscience. (Of the Korean War, the *New York Herald Tribune* remarked, "Truman lost his temper, MacArthur lost his job, Acheson lost the war, a million and half Koreans lost their lives, and Stalin didn't lose a night's sleep.") But as the rain falls on the just and the unjust alike, the lessons of history issue from the sane and the insane alike.

"Whoever holds a power but newly gained is ever stern of mood," wrote Aeschylus twenty-five hundred years ago, and nothing much has happened to lighten things up. Note the next time a new CEO is announced at a large public corporation. Within a few weeks several key executives of the company will announce they are leaving "to pursue other interests." Their axings have biblical precedent, and as usual the biblical account is a lot bloodier.

Five hundred years before Aeschylus—around 1000 B.C.—the kingdom of Israel was at peace, and King David was in slow decline. As the infirm king lay in his palace, his oldest surviving son, Adonijah, took on more and more the mantle of royal prerogative. He moved about Jerusalem in a great chariot, accompanied by his own guards. Joab, the fearsome commander of David's army, openly supported the prince, and it seemed to all that an orderly transition would take place on David's death.

But the prophet Nathan did not want Adonijah to inherit this kingdom of God's chosen people. He had long watched these sons of the king, and he had decided on Adonijah's younger half-brother Solomon, son of Bathsheba. Solomon had special gifts his older sibling did not possess. Nathan had decided Solomon should rule Israel.

The key to all the events that would soon ensue would depend, strangely enough, on a young country girl named Abishag of Shunam. She had been chosen from among all the girls in Israel to serve the king in his old age, and our only description of her is that she was "very beautiful." Through no effort or fault of her own she was also very powerful at a very delicate time. Her position at the faltering king's side meant she controlled who saw the king. Access—then as now—was all-important.

One day Adonijah threw a banquet for his supporters, and quite naturally many toasts were made celebrating his coming accession to the throne. Jerusalem now is a small city and it was even smaller then, so it was no surprise that the party drew Nathan's attention. He saw the celebrating and heard the toasting. He knew for certain that David, holding on to power to the very end, could not have named Adonijah as his successor, and that he would be incensed at the presumption. This was the moment, and Nathan moved fast. He went straight to Bathsheba and Solomon.

Everything now depended on Abishag of Shunam. Certainly an old man like Nathan was not the right person to try to see the king. Someone should go whom the girl would allow into the king's presence. Who better than an older woman, and who better among women than the king's still-beloved Bathsheba?

So Bathsheba went to the king's rooms. The girl admitted her, and now we must suspect some collusion between Bathsheba the wife and Abishag the concubine, because in Abishag's presence Bathsheba told David of Adonijah's feast and the toasts that were being made. She put the question to the old warrior point-blank, the way soldiers like it. Had he named Adonijah king? And if he had, what was to become of her and Solomon once Adonijah took power? At that moment (and here our suspicion of collusion rises to a new level) Nathan himself entered into the room. He asked his old friend the king the same questions.

The old king rallied. His clingings to the throne had now become too dangerous. Displaying once again the decisiveness that had gained him the kingdom, he ordered the prophet Nathan to summon the priests and take Solomon down to the place of anointing and with trumpets proclaim him king.

The hastily ordered procession of the priests, with their cymbals and loud prayers, created noise of its own, and some of Adonijah's party-goers wandered out to see what the commotion was. When they learned what King David had ordered, they fled in terror. Adonijah himself ran from his house to the sanctuary of the altar, where by custom no harm could be done to him. The newly anointed King Solomon was told of his brother's flight to sanctuary. He sent a message to his brother to go home and to cause no trouble.

Now Solomon was brought before the dying king. From his deathbed, father instructed son on the ruthlessness it takes to rule a nation. The first step must be to eliminate Joab. As commander of the army, Joab held too much power, which he would use against the teenage king. Next to die must be Shimei of Saul's clan, the last remaining claimant of the old royal family that David had usurped so many years ago. David had sworn Shimei could live in peace, but that was David's promise, not Solomon's. The old king went on to instruct Solomon on whom he could trust and who should be rewarded. With his instruction in the bloody arts of kingship done, the old monarch died.

The prince Adonijah seems to have mistaken Solomon's leniency toward him for weakness. Unaware that execution squads were moving through the city at the king's command, he decided to risk a subtle move. The prince visited Bathsheba. The kingdom should have been his, he said bluntly, but he would accept that God's favor rested on Solomon. The king only had to grant him one thing, and all would be well. Bathsheba asked Adonijah what he wanted. Only one thing, he responded, and that is to have Abishag of Shunam as his wife.

Bathsheba seems to have thought this a good solution. Abishag had proven her loyalty. Perhaps as the wife of Adonijah she could help bring his partisans to Solomon's side. Whatever her reasoning, she decided to go to Solomon with Adonijah's request.

But Solomon had learned well at his father's deathbed. Adonijah was attempting too clever a move. If he obtained the hand of Abishag, David's virgin queen, it would be seen as tantamount to establishing a parallel kingship. Solomon did not hesitate. Within the hour Adonijah was seized and put to death.

Of Abishag of Shunam nothing more is known. The biblical account tells us Solomon had seven hundred wives and three hundred concubines. We can assume that Abishag of Shunam held a place of honor among them.

But of Solomon we can be sure. Nineteen years old on assuming the throne, he left no doubt in anyone's mind that he meant to keep it. He did, for another forty years.

▶ **Remember: Power is not a game of patty-cake. For three thousand years the world has marveled at the "wisdom of Solomon"—one of the greatest kings who ever reigned. His first and greatest act of** wisdom was to recognize the play against him, and to move swiftly to cut it off.

The Emperor Who Kowtowed

Appear to submit, then prepare to win

In mandarin China the *k'o-t'ou,* or kowtow, was ritual respect shown to a superior by formally kneeling and touching the forehead to the ground. Not too many of us are so obsequious when we walk into our boss's office, but there is not one of us who has not at one time performed a modern equivalent of a kowtow, even if it's only saying "yes, sir" through clenched teeth.

The plain fact is, there are moments when every one of us has to yield the field, and sometimes we have to do it in front of colleagues, friends, or family. Of course, these can become moments of high historical drama, as when Lee offered his sword to Grant at Appomattox (the embarrassed Union general refused to take it) or when the Japanese formally surrendered on the U.S.S. *Missouri.* But formal submission is not just for those who have lost a war. The kowtow can sometimes be a useful device to those who mean to win one.

Hildebrand of Tuscany had served eight popes for twenty-five years before his own election to the papacy as Gregory VII on April 22, 1073 (he was ordained a priest the same day). Through his long years of service he had developed a deep hostility toward the twin evils of simony and lay investiture that infected and corrupted the Church of his time. He came to the throne of St. Peter determined to wipe out both of them, and he went about his mission with such ferocity that his contemporaries nicknamed him "Hellbrand."

Simony, or the sale of Church offices (named for Simon

Magus, the magician who in Acts tries to buy his way into becoming an apostle), was a favorite method of raising money for the war-loving, cash-starved princelings of Europe. The practice was so common, and attempts to end it so frequent and futile, that Philip I of France once remarked to a disappointed suitor for a local bishopric, "Let me earn my profit from your rival. Then have the man indicted for simony, and I'll let you buy it."

The king's flippant attitude toward the holy orders outraged the growing number of reformers who saw lay investiture as the crux of the problem. Over the centuries the feudal system had slowly enveloped the Church. By Hildebrand's time it had come to be considered good and proper custom that a bishop, who was supposed to be elected by the local clergy, would instead be handpicked by the ruling lord, who would then invest him with his ring as a symbol of his marriage to the diocese. In the minds of most of the populace it was this ritual act that *made* someone a bishop. In the minds of some of the nobility it was an easy way to add to the treasury. Greed pervaded the system and degraded the Church, and Hildebrand—now Pope Gregory VII, later Saint Gregory VII—meant to put a stop to it.

In 1075 the new pope called a synod in Rome which denounced simony and lay investiture as crimes. He then promptly made good on the synod's decrees by deposing five bishops who were known to have bought their offices.

Those five bishops happened to be councillors to Henry IV, the Holy Roman emperor. He was not amused. To show what he thought of this new idea, he appointed an archbishop to the vacant see of Milan, almost under the pope's nose. Henry had every reason to believe that this demonstration of power would end the matter. After all, the imperial family had a history of dethroning troublemaking popes (Henry's father had deposed three popes and named four). Besides, custom was on his side, and, since he had chosen them, he could count on a large number of bishops to back him up in council.

Instead he received a written remonstrance from Gregory, ordering him to stop the practice once and for all. Enraged, the emperor sent his own letter to Gregory, deposing him as pope.

Gregory replied by excommunicating Henry, deposing him as emperor, and advising the world that all feudal oaths to the former emperor were no longer valid.

Pope Gregory's action was, to put it mildly, the direct opposite of lay investiture. Nothing like it had ever been done before. It immediately generated a Europe-wide furor. To top it off, the pope announced that he would come to Germany to preside over a council which would elect a new Holy Roman emperor.

Henry's enemies were delighted, and his friends were suddenly scarce. The bishops who had advised him instantly discovered urgent business back in their dioceses. Saxony erupted in revolt, the emperor's emissaries to other courts were brusquely turned away, and his nobles declared in their own council that Henry must step down. The pope, it seems, had unleashed a tidal wave of pent-up resentment over the arrogance of imperial rule.

Henry may have been arrogant, but he was nobody's fool. With a small retinue he immediately headed for Italy. He intercepted Gregory en route to Germany at Canossa, the castle of the Countess Matilda of Tuscany, high in the Apennines. There the emperor presented himself at the gate barefoot, donned in sackcloth, and covered with ashes. For three days, during one of the worst winters in memory, he knelt in the snow, publicly begging the Vicar of Christ for absolution.

The pope recognized that Henry had put him in a quandary. If he absolved the penitent emperor, Henry could declare the forthcoming council unnecessary, resume his office, and proceed to take vengeance on all who had opposed him. On the other hand, if Gregory denied absolution to the man kneeling in the snow he would be violating his duty as a priest.

Finally Gregory had no choice. He granted absolution to Henry, who took off like a bat out of hell, just as the pope had feared he would.

Seven years later the emperor crossed the Alps into Italy again—this time with an army. He besieged Rome, deposed Gregory as pope, and installed his own antipope in his place.

Gregory's reforms would eventually win out, and the independence of the Church would be restored. But Henry had shown that even an emperor can make good use of knowing when to kowtow.

▶ Remember: Losing face is less important than gaining your goal, and sometimes it can help you do it.

How to Treat a Desperate Foe

Never back an opponent into a corner from which he cannot retreat

By all accounts the most dangerous animal on earth is a bear that's been run up a tree. The ferocious glint in the eyes means certain trouble. That glint is not restricted to bears, as anyone who has ever cut the legs out from under a colleague's arguments across a conference room table knows. A committed opponent who is left with no choice will frequently attack rather than surrender, usually just at the moment when you expect the flutter of a white flag.

The famous strategist Sun-tzu tells the story of the Chinese general Fu Yeng-ch'ing, who made an expedition against the Khitans in 945 B.C. As his army traversed bare and desertlike ground, it was ambushed. The general quickly threw up a defensive perimeter and managed to hold off the attack, but he found himself completely surrounded. Soon his men were scrounging for any water they could find; the wells they had dug ran dry, and they were reduced to squeezing lumps of mud from the wells to suck out the moisture. As the enemy pressed a series of attacks from all sides, Fu Yeng-ch'ing's soldiers began to falter, then die; the general watched helplessly as the torrid heat did his enemy's work. Finally one afternoon a strong gale started up from the northeast, producing a massive sandstorm. The enemy decided to hold off its final attack until the sandstorm died down. A Chinese officer saw the opportunity, and appealed to the general, "We are now few and they are many, but in the midst of this sandstorm our numbers will not be discernible. Victory will go to surprise and fierceness." Accordingly, Fu Yeng-ch'ing gathered what was left of his army and, with the wind at his back, led a sudden attack on the southwest position of the enemy. He routed the force in front of him, then wheeled into the wind to destroy the remaining Khitans.

Montaigne relates a similar story about an army loyal to Julius Caesar that found itself besieged at Solana by Pompey's general Marcus Octavius in 46 B.C. Octavius made it a condition that to lift the siege the soldiers had to forswear their allegiance to Caesar; from inside the walls the loyal veterans of Caesar's Gallic Wars replied they would never surrender under that condition. The siege dragged on for months; the water supply to the town was cut off, and provisions were exhausted. Outside the walls the surrounding army had nothing to do but wait. Inside the walls every day was a desperate struggle to survive. Those who only wait tend to relax and become careless; those who struggle become hardened and even more determined. Finally, on a chosen day, about noon, the defenders stripped themselves of their armor, buckled it on the women and children, and placed them in the guard positions around the walls. Just as the enemy was settling down to its accustomed noon meal, the gates suddenly opened and Caesar's veterans poured out, attacking so furiously that they routed the first, second, and third outer posts, and then the fourth, then overran all the entrenchments, forcing the enemy to flee to its ships. Octavius barely escaped with his life.

The familiar story of the Alamo shows that even a victory in such a situation can be ruinous. In 1836 the Mexican dictator Santa Anna laid siege with an army of five thousand to the tiny band of Texans at the old mission in San Antonio. For nearly two weeks his artillery battered away at the sturdy mission walls with little result. Meanwhile, miles away, Sam Houston was hurriedly gathering from every town and farm a force to meet the Mexican general's punitive expedition. When Santa Anna finally called on the Alamo defenders one last time to surrender, their commander,

Colonel William Travis, replied with a cannonball. Santa Anna's response to Travis' deliberate provocation was to fall for it. Instead of merely bypassing the little outpost to pursue the major concentration of Texans rallying to Sam Houston, Santa Anna ordered his trumpeters to sound the "Diablo," the Mexican signal that no quarter would be given. To the Texans inside, this meant they had no choice but to fight to the death, which they did for another crucial three days. After finally annihilating the Texans, Santa Anna marched on to San Jacinto, where his exhausted and bloodied army was surprised and easily overcome by Houston.

Contrast Santa Anna's military strategy with John F. Kennedy's political strategy during the Cuban missile crisis of 1962. Records of the meetings show that Kennedy spent little time on such matters as the correlation of forces, military pressure points, and other tactical concerns. Rather, almost every moment was taken up with the critical strategic question of how to leave open a path of retreat for the Soviets so that Khrushchev could back down without losing face.

Kennedy was following the wisdom of Sun-tzu as laid down some twenty-five hundred years ago: "When you surround an enemy, leave an outlet free. This does not mean that the enemy is to be allowed to escape. The object is to make him believe that there is a road to safety, and thus prevent his fighting with the courage of despair." Those who were alive in 1962 will remember how close the United States was to an all-out nuclear war over Cuba. The lesson to remember is how it was avoided.

▶ Remember: A committed foe about to suffer defeat is more dangerous than ever before. Always let him believe he has a way out, to prevent him from turning on you with the full force of desperate ferocity.

The Scholar Who
Tamed the Vikings

Win a defeated opponent over to your side, thereby winning twice

Bad losers may get the rap, but bad winners are the ones who deserve it. Okay, so sometimes bad manners are justified. After a game in which the other side fouled and cheated, what winner isn't tempted to deliver a less polite version of "So there!"

Nations get as carried away as people. After the Civil War and Lincoln's assassination, the North brutally repressed the South and sank an already ravaged economy, which acted as a drag on national growth for another hundred years. Maybe that taught us a lesson, because we dealt generously with Japan and Germany after World War II, igniting not only a postwar boom but also weaving democratic values into the fabric of their nations' political cultures.

But who learns from history? The Congress of Vienna in 1815 successfully restored a defeated France into the family of nations. A hundred years later that example was either forgotten or ignored. The Treaty of Versailles after World War I stomped a defeated Germany into the ground, making it a restless cauldron waiting to boil over.

Stupidities such as Reconstruction and the Treaty of Versailles are repeated every day on a thousand different fields. Companies wage battles to take each other over, then the winner sets out systematically to destroy the very culture that made the other company worth battling for. In ancient history, and almost alone in all of history, are the Romans, who left the peoples they conquered to themselves as much as possible. The great thing about the Romans was their consistency: they didn't care about anything other than the tax revenue.

By the ninth century the only people who could learn this valuable lesson from the Romans were people who could read, and those people were few. Literacy was kept alive only in monasteries, and those sacred places naturally concentrated their attention on sacred texts. So it was fortunate that the youngest of the five sons of the King of Wessex in that bloody century was tutored as a youth and learned to read. And it is perhaps more fortunate, at least for England as we know it and those nations that were spawned by it, that this studious young man taught himself Latin, loved libraries, and yearned to read more than was respectable for a prince. He studied the sacred texts, of course; but he also delved into the interesting histories of Rome.

The Vikings had begun their incursions into England in the 790s, and by the 850s had established such control with their settlements in the northern and eastern parts that they could enforce the imposition of their rules, customs, and language, called Danelaw. The Anglo-Saxon resistance had been overcome by the fierce warrior code of the invaders, much as the Anglo-Saxons themselves had overwhelmed the native Britons four centuries before. Nothing seemed to be able to withstand these invaders, and anything in their path that mounted a resistance—town, monastery, fortress—was totally destroyed.

Meanwhile, Alfred was reading. While Alfred was reading, his brothers were dying, as attempt after attempt failed against the power of the Vikings. In January 871, Alfred left his books to join his last remaining brother in yet another battle, which was won by a surprise attack planned by the young scholar. When that brother died, Alfred was named ruler of a kingdom that looked to be on its last legs.

For the next seven years the new king did what he could do to buy time. Sometimes he paid tribute to Viking chieftains to keep them at bay. Meanwhile, in secret camps, he trained Wessex men in the arts of harassment, which we now call guerrilla warfare. These small but damaging affronts to the Vikings' vaunted invincibility inflicted more than physical damage on the proud invaders; they showed vulnerability.

Meanwhile, the Vikings kept chipping away, steadily ravaging the land, moving closer into the heartland of Alfred's kingdom. The test came in 877, when the Vikings decided to take Wessex and therefore be done with it. To their surprise, Alfred offered no resistance. They invaded as far as the capital city, Winchester, and by some accounts razed it to the ground. His refusal to meet them head-on apparently enraged the enemy, who plunged deeper into Wessex to root him out. On Christmas Day, they almost surprised Alfred at Mass in Chippenham but the alarm was sounded, and he quickly fell back to the marshes. Having lured the enemy so far into the English interior, Alfred now sent out a call to all freeborn men in the neighboring shires of Somerset, Wiltshire, and Hampshire. Even Alfred must have been surprised by the numbers his royal summons produced at the moment his royalty was most in doubt.

The trained Wessex fighters and their new volunteers attacked the Viking encampment at Edington on a crisp day in January 878. All day the fierce battle raged high on the Downs, but the English were unrelenting. More important, they employed Roman infantry tactics that Alfred had discovered in one of his books and which the Vikings had never seen. By evening the enemy survivors were desperately trying to hold the inner perimeter of their own camp.

The next morning should have produced a massacre; the Wessex men had many scores to settle. Instead it began with a white flag from the English side. In the place of certain death, Alfred offered the Vikings a deal. If they agreed to accept baptism as Christians and disband what was left of their Great Army, they could continue to practice Danelaw in the land they held, but only as Alfred's subjects. The exhausted Vikings were astonished. To keep what they had gained, plus their lives, they need only accept Alfred's God and Alfred's reign. They agreed.

Alfred made sure the acceptance was real. He required that the Vikings and his own men remain until Easter in one place, living next to one another. He required that his men teach the enemy their language and their religion, and—the monastery never far away from Alfred's mind—accept them as brothers. Amazingly enough, they did, and it worked. Alfred enforced his kingship for the next eight years. In 886 he beseiged and won London.

Other Vikings tried various smaller attacks on Alfred, but he had taken the steam out of the invasion. As overlord he ruled most of the Viking territory without ever setting foot in it. Soon fierce invaders became settlers who wanted the same stability for their children that Alfred had established for his subjects. What the English king could never have gained by force, considering the meagerness of his resources and the strength of his enemy, he had gained by peace.

Alfred never proclaimed himself King of all England. He didn't see the point in offending chieftains with hereditary rights while gaining nothing but a title. Nevertheless, by the time of his death he was regarded by everyone as ruler of the nation. He is the only monarch in English history to be called "the Great."

▶ **Remember: Bill Gates didn't destroy a humbled Apple; he invested in it. A competitor need not be an enemy, and an enemy need not remain one. By winning over a defeated opponent, you have the opportunity to win twice.**

The Daughter-in-Law Who Played the Prostitute

Use your opponent's desires or fears

Deception is the oldest tactic in the book—after all, the snake used it on Eve.

The Greeks used it on the Trojans. When they rolled their huge Trojan Horse up to the gates of Troy, then pretended to head for their ships to return home, they were counting on the Trojans' hope that the bloody ten-year war had finally come to an end.

A deception is not a lie, exactly. Rather it is more of a ruse, a stratagem intended to mislead. Saying "John lied to me" is different than saying "John led me to believe . . ." In one case, the fault lies with John; in the other, it lies partly with me. After all, who was responsible for the apple being eaten, the snake or Eve?

A thousand stories could be told of mankind's use of tricks.

Julius Caesar was a master of deception, and so was the upright Robert E. Lee. For several months Lee fooled Union commander George McClellan into believing that the South's army was as big or bigger than his. Despite telegram after telegram from Lincoln urging him to attack, McClellan was afraid of an engagement that might lose him his army. Eighty years after Lee, preparing for the biggest gamble of his life, Eishenhower set up a dummy army complete with cardboard tanks—with George Patton in nominal command—to convince Hitler that the long-expected invasion of Europe was coming against Calais and not Normandy.

Deception is common enough in warfare, but is also useful in emergencies, as when the Scottish hero William Wallace was once surrounded by English troops searching for him. He quickly donned women's clothes and flounced his way past them without attracting even a suspicious glance.

Japanese plays, puppet shows, and folk dances have long celebrated an incident in which the hero-warrior Yoshitsune of the great clan Minamoto was fleeing the wrath of his half-brother, the shogun. Yoshitsune was the object of the most relentless and organized manhunt in Japanese history; all ports were closed, all roads were blocked. Yoshitsune and his small band dressed as common laborers, carrying baskets on their backs like the humblest coolies. Led by Yoshitsune's stalwart companion, Benkei, the band encountered a barricade on the road to Akita. Benkei approached the guards' commander and was refused passage. He protested that they were actually a group of monks in disguise, and in these dangerous times they needed to get back to their monastery. He even managed to quote a Buddhist adage or two to that effect. The commander looked suspiciously at Yoshitsune, whose noble mien was undisguised by dirty clothes. Benkei immediately began beating and verbally abusing the great warrior in a manner no noble Minamoto would ever have tolerated. The guards let them pass.

One deception with farther-reaching consequences was committed by a woman to regain her honor. It also gained her a place in the patriarchal history of three great religions.

Tamar was chosen by Judah, the son of Jacob and the great-grandson of Abraham, to wed the firstborn of his three sons, Er.

Soon after the marriage Er died ("he was wicked in the sight of the Lord; and the Lord slew him," the Bible tells us). By custom—and later, law—the second son was obligated to marry his brother's widow and produce children, who would then be considered sons of the firstborn, endowed with all the rights of primogeniture. But Onan, the second son, didn't much like the idea of having his children raised as his brother's. He dutifully went to Tamar's bed, but withdrew at the climactic moment ("he spilled it on the ground, lest that he should give seed to his brother"). For this lack of cooperation, Onan too died ("and the thing which he did displeased the Lord: wherefore he slew him").

Judah now had only one son left, and he was understandably concerned about letting Tamar near him. With the excuse that this third son, Shelah, needed to grow up a little before fulfilling his fraternal duty, he sent Tamar back to her father's house to live as a widow.

Time passed, Shelah came of age, and still no word came from Judah. Tamar began to feel she was being duped. Two could play that game.

One day Tamar received word that Judah was going to Timnath for the annual sheep-shearing. She shed her widow's garments, donned a veil and wrapped herself in it, and sat in an open place on the road to Timnath. When Judah came by he saw her, and presuming her to be a prostitute, asked her price. Tamar asked how much he was willing to pay. Judah said that he would send her a sheep from his flock. That's fine, Tamar replied, but how do I know you'll send it? What do you want? asked Judah. Tamar suggested that he leave his signet, his bracelets, and his staff with her to be redeemed when the sheep arrived. Judah agreed. After their dalliance, Tamar went back home, removed the veil, and put back on her widow's outfit.

Judah sent a friend with a sheep to redeem his pledge, but the friend couldn't find the prostitute. He asked around the neighborhood, but was told no prostitute had ever been there. He went back and reported this to Judah. Both of them must have shrugged their shoulders.

About three months later Judah was told his daughter-in-law

was pregnant. Outraged because she was still supposed to be married to his son, he summoned her. This was the moment Tamar had been waiting for. She presented the signet, the bracelets, and the staff, and said, "By the man whose these are, am I with child." While that sank in, she asked (one imagines very sweetly), "Whose are these, the signet, and bracelets, and staff?" Abashed at his own failure to obey the custom, Judah declared, "She has been more righteous than I."

Tamar's twin boys by Judah, Pharez and Zarah, were to be the progenitors of the great tribe of Judah, which was to become the Jewish people. They owe their existence not only to the patriarchs, but also to the clever ruse of a strong woman.

▶ Remember: Deception only works when it plays to your opponent's desires or fears. Lee used it against McClellan but not against Grant. Tamar's worked on Judah because he was abashed by his own failure to follow tribal tradition. His embarrassment was her opportunity.

The Princess Who Stole the Silkworm

Keep your secrets to yourself

Coca-Cola keeps the four-page recipe that made it the world's best-selling soft drink in a bank vault in downtown Atlanta, where it has rested for one hundred years. Only two executives are allowed to know what it is. Kentucky Fried Chicken keeps the Colonel's original recipe with its eleven herbs and spices in a time capsule at an undisclosed, guarded location. ("I could tell you where it is," a company spokesman told the *Washington Times*' Anne Marriott, "but then I'd have to kill you.") In a case that rocked the international automotive industry, General Motors accused a former executive of stealing trade secrets when he resigned to join Volkswagen, and pursued him and his new company in court.

Secrets are serious business. In the 1930s Hedy Lamarr was a young German film star married to an Austrian munitions manufacturer. Unknown to her husband, she was also an underground anti-Nazi. When her husband was commissioned to find a way to use radio signals to guide torpedoes to their targets, his lovely wife insisted on traveling with him to meetings in Berlin to discuss the project. Welcomed for her beauty and fame—she was no doubt that decade's version of the trophy wife—she listened as Nazi scientists and naval officials pondered aloud the problems with radio. The major problem was that radio signals can be jammed, so the project centered on frequency hopping, a method of jumping around the dial that could only be read by the intended receiver and not by outside listeners. Ms. Lamarr silently soaked up every detail.

One night she drugged her maid to keep her from raising the alarm, escaped from home, and followed a prearranged route through Austria to London, where she was met by Louis Mayer, the Hollywood studio head. In Washington she debriefed the U.S. Navy on German intentions, and, after some further work at its request, in 1942 filed a secret patent on frequency hopping for wartime communications. Neither the patent nor Ms. Lamarr's espionage was revealed until a report in *Forbes* magazine in 1990. The Germans never knew that the movie star with the beautiful face also possessed a beautiful mind.

The most closely guarded trade secret ever, measured by how long it was kept a secret, was the Chinese invention of the manufacture of silk. The silkworm (which is really a caterpillar) is native to China, and the discovery of its potential goes back into the mists of history. Tradition credits Si Ling-chi, the fourteen-year-old bride of the Emperor Huang Ti, with the invention of the silk reel, which would place its first use as a material to sometime around 2550 B.C.

The silkworm remained a secret for the next thirty centuries. Torture and beheadings were regularly prescribed for those who even dared mention the worm's existence. Border stations were established at every possible entry into China, and maintained around-the-clock with guards who searched every parcel of every traveler.

The trouble was well worth it. Silk was a source of incredible wealth for China and its emperors. The great trade routes over the Tien Shan and Kunlun mountain ranges were traversed by caravans carrying bolts of the precious fabric to the courts of Asia and the Middle East. When Darius III surrendered to Alexander the Great in 331 B.C. he clothed himself in such a splendid array of silk that Alexander was completely overshadowed. In a huff Alexander demanded as tribute the equivalent of seven million dollars' worth of silk for himself.

The southern trade route skirted the great Gobi Desert and went through the small oasis kingdom of Khotan. By the time of the Chin dynasty in China, the little kingdom had seen generations of wealth pass through the portals of its city, and finally its kings could no longer stand it. The story of how Khotan stole China's most valuable asset is recounted by Hsuan Tsang, a Buddhist Chinese who visited Khotan in the seventh century.

The kings of Khotan had tried many times to get their cousins, the emperors of China, to divulge the secret of silk, and each time had been politely rebuffed. This king decided to try another tactic. He sent his emissary to the Chinese court and requested that in recognition of the long respect that had existed between the two monarchies the emperor consent to send one of his daughters to Khotan as a bride for its king. This was an established practice of Chinese diplomacy, and the emperor happily agreed.

On meeting the young princess the king's emissary counseled her that Khotan was a faraway country and that she would undoubtedly never see her homeland again. If she wanted to lay the foundations for a harmonious married life and to enjoy the fine silk robes she was so accustomed to wearing, she had better bring the means for making them.

The ingenious princess arranged for a tour of a local silkworm farm, and during the course of her inspection managed to slip some silkworms and mulberry seeds into a pocket. When the royal caravan departed to take her to Khotan, she hid the contraband in her headdress, which the frontier guards naturally did not have the impertinence to examine.

In Khotan the princess founded the Lu-she convent, where the silkworms were bred, and some three hundred years later Hsuan Tsang was proudly shown the mulberry trees said to have grown from the seeds she had filched. A painted panel of the princess with her headdress was discovered by the great archaeologist Sir Aurel Stein on one of his expeditions in the 1930s and now hangs in the British Museum.

By the time Hsuan visited the tiny kingdom in 644 A.D. silk was its principal export. Unfortunately, little Khotan was absorbed by China in the seventeenth century. But then, of course, it was much too late to protect the secret of the silkworm.

▶ **Remember: Even most innocent-appearing people—a movie star, perhaps, or a young princess—may have their own purposes in mind. Guard your secrets well.**

part three

SETTING YOUR OWN AGENDA

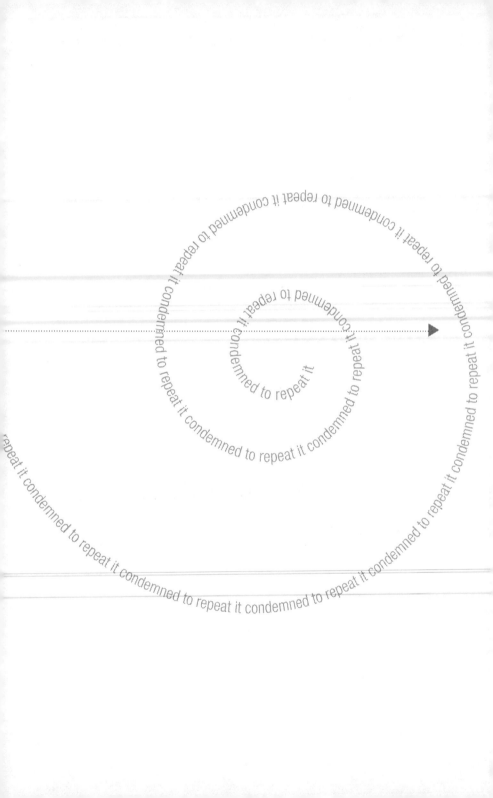

The Bulb That Broke a Nation

Don't follow the herd

For years Winston Churchill was a lonely voice warning about Nazi intentions and arguing for rearmament, but to no avail. He was ridiculed in the press, shouted down in the House of Commons, and ignored by the government. But when war came, and England stood alone, Churchill became a war leader and mobilized the nation. In January 1942 a vote of confidence in Churchill's leadership passed in the House of Commons by a margin of 464–1. The lonely dissenter was shunned by the members, but as Churchill was leaving the House he took the man by the arm. "Be of good cheer," he whispered. "If recent history is any guide, you will one day be prime minister of England."

Standing alone against the crowd is not easy, especially when money is at stake. A young lady in the 1950s approached the renowned financier Bernard Baruch at a party. "My trustees have invested a part of my portfolio in a small company," she said. "My friends think the investment is stupid." Baruch didn't even inquire into the name of the company. "If your friends think it is stupid, my advice is that you keep it." The stock was in a little company called IBM. Baruch, of course, didn't know the stock was IBM, and no doubt wouldn't have had an opinion if he had known. He simply distrusted "friends."

"All economic movements," Baruch had written earlier, "are by their very nature motivated by crowd psychology." Maybe that's why on the stock exchange, bulls symbolize an up market and bears a down market: bulls move in herds, and bears slink away by themselves.

In the Amsterdam of 1634 the biggest market wasn't in stocks—it was in tulips.

A Dutchman by the name of Conrad Gesner first came upon the tulip in a nobleman's garden in Augsburg in 1559. The baron had received the plant as a gift from an acquaintance in Constantinople (its name is thought to come from the Turkish word for turban). Following his pleasant discovery in the German nobleman's garden, Gesner and an increasingly wide circle of his aristocratic friends began ordering bulbs directly from Constantinople at very expensive prices—in the world's first documented case of mail order.

As the flowers began to be seen more and more in the gardens of the best houses in Amsterdam, more and more of the best people wanted to have them. By the early 1630s it became the hallmark of a Dutch gentleman to have his own collection of tulips.

When the upper classes latch on to something, the aspiring middle classes aren't far behind. By 1634 tulips were all the rage among the prudent Dutch: the entire country seemed to have thrown over its old occupations to engage in the tulip trade. The spiraling demand depleted bulb stocks, and prices soared. With every increase in price, the demand grew. At the end of the year, in a country where a well-bred ox cost 120 florins, a single tulip of the species *Admiral liefken* sold for 4,400 florins. A less noble *Childer* went for 1,615 florins, while a precious *Semper augustus* was a bargain at 5,500 florins.

The rest of the world remained curiously unaware of the Dutch craze. In *Popular Delusions*, published in 1841, London journalist Charles MacKay recounts the story of a shipmaster who one morning unloaded his consignment of goods from the Middle East to a well-known Amsterdam merchant and as a matter of courtesy was invited to breakfast. While the merchant was out of the room, the sailor noticed a nice-looking onion on the table, which he sliced up and ate as a fitting compliment to his herring. The "onion" turned out to be a *Semper augustus.* To his amazement and the merchant's utter bereavement, he soon learned his breakfast condiment could have outfitted his entire ship's crew for a year.

Where there is value, there is a human tendency to speculate. Soon tulip spotters were plying the alleys and byways of Holland looking for new varieties or species with even the slightest mutation. Tulips were entered on the Amsterdam and Rotterdam stock exchanges, and two years later on the London Exchange as well.

Everyone, from the richest to the poorest, began to dabble in tulips; the smallest properties were converted to cash, great estates were sold at rock-bottom prices, businesses were liquidated—all to allow their owners to get their hands on more tulips. Special laws were passed to identify the major species and to regulate their trade.

By the end of 1636 it finally became too expensive to own a tulip for its beauty. Even the very rich had their gardens dug up so that the bulbs could be sold on the exchanges. The upper classes who had started the craze were no longer buyers; they were sellers. When this was noticed, prices fell a little—and never recovered. Within a month, tulip prices took a nosedive. Thousands of people found themselves under contract to buy tulips at the old price. Lawsuits multiplied, and bankruptcies filled the courts. A special commission of dealers attempted to halt the collapse by ordering the contracts renegotiated, but this failed. The government attempted to intervene, but found itself powerless. The florin itself was destabilized. A general depression ensued.

A tulip, it turned out, was only a tulip.

▶ **Remember: When everyone else is charging full-speed in one direction, you should cast an appraising eye in the other.**

The Slave and the Seven-Year Wait

Knock over the table

Life is a lot like gin rummy. You have only three choices: win the hand you're dealt, wait for the next shuffle, or knock over the table.

Too few of us are willing to break out of the ruts we're in, as if our position in life was established by some immutable law and we're stuck with it. At an abolitionist meeting in Boston in 1843 Frederick Douglass was making a pessimistic speech about the possibility of ever ending slavery. Suddenly from the audience an old black woman named Sojourner Truth rose from her seat and cried, "Is God dead?" Douglass had handled many a heckler, but the impassioned cry left him momentarily speechless. The audience didn't stir. At first tentatively and then with a great wave, applause rocked the auditorium.

God wasn't dead to Harriet Jacobs. She was a slave who was supposed to have been free, and she was not about to accept the accidental difference.

Long before Harriet was born, her grandmother and great-uncles had been manumitted by their father, a "white gentleman," and sent to Spanish Florida, but the ship on which they were sailing was captured by an American Revolutionary naval vessel, and the captain had sold them back into slavery. Harriet's own father, another "white gentleman," had made a comparable promise, but never kept it. The father of Harriet's two children, a neighbor of her owners and a distinguished local figure who was eventually elected to Congress, made more promises, but let them languish. (The sexual exploitation of slave women seems to have been as common as the promises.)

The final straw for Harriet came when her mistress died. Once again, she had been promised freedom, but the will contained no such provision. Worse, her mistress' death left her at the mercy of the husband, whose cruelty had been kept in bounds by his wife. He tormented Harriet, perhaps frustrated by her liaison with his prominent neighbor, and finally announced he would "break in" her son and daughter (then ages six and four) to the brutalized life of field workers.

Harried believed she had no choice but to escape. She knew she couldn't flee with two young children, so she counted on her grandmother to provide protection until she could send for them. On her first night out, while hiding in the woods, she was bitten in the leg by a poisonous snake. She crawled back to the slave quarters, alerted her grandmother, and concealed herself in a tiny hidden room built into the eaves of her grandmother's cottage. In that cramped space she could barely move or stand up. But the physical discomfort was nothing compared to the emotional anguish, for everyday she could hear the sounds of her children playing below her, unaware that their mother was secreted only a few feet away. Incredibly, she endured her pain in that little closet for seven years—which by the time she was able to escape, was nearly one fourth of her life. This was a woman who wanted to be free.

In 1842 Harriet finally saw an opportunity, came down from her hiding spot, and, by traveling at night through isolated regions, fled north to the free states. Once settled in New York she managed, miraculously enough, to extricate her children from slavery and through the connivance of other slaves have them brought north. But her dangers weren't over. A fugitive slave was still a slave, and many states like New York, while free themselves, were unsympathetic to the idea of stolen property—even if the property in this case had stolen herself. (New York would remain a hotbed of pro-South sentiment during the Civil War.) A relative of her employer threatened to denounce Harriet to the authorities; that night she packed up her children and fled across the river to Brooklyn. She found another job, but when the federal Fugitive Slave Law was passed in 1850, she fled once again, this time to pro-abolitionist Boston, where she appealed for help. The Colonization Society took up her cause, raised money, and finally purchased Harriet and her children from the doubtlessly even more frustrated owner, who had no chance at recouping his loss any other way.

As improbable as Harriet's journey to freedom was, she was guided by an unshakable faith that freedom was her destiny. As she explains in her autobiography, *Incidents in the Life of a Slave Girl*, for herself and for the grandmother who raised her, American blacks were the new people of Israel, entrapped in Egyptian slavery, yearning for deliverance, and praying to God for an eventual escape to the Promised Land.

Harriet Jacobs never found a Moses, so she crossed the Red Sea by herself.

Everyone has a Red Sea. And many are sitting on the shore waiting for any Moses that will come along. Not Harriet Jacobs, whose name in time may become as famous as any in American history—not because she was a slave girl, but because she believed by right she was as free as any women ever born.

▶ **Remember: Neither your present station in life nor your future success or failure is set in stone. Your character and your determination are your future. Use them to shape it. If you don't like the cards you've been dealt, go ahead: knock over that table.**

The Oath That Killed Achilles

Make promises carefully, and be sure to keep them

In the middle of the eleventh century three schoolboys in the city of Nishapur in eastern Persia swore an oath that whoever achieved the greatest success would help the other two. One of the boys proved so capable that he rose to become grand vizier to the sultan. The second of the boys was inclined toward scholarship, and his friend the grand vizier secured him a professorship; an exceptional mathematician, he is better known for his melancholy poems collected in *The Rubáiyát of Omar Khayyám*. The third boy was a troublemaker, and once when in serious difficulty he approached his old friend the grand vizier for help. To his surprise, he was brusquely rejected. Hassan-i Sabbah was not a man to endure a slight, and he soon formed his own cult—the Order of the Assassins*—to take revenge on his enemies. His first target in 1092 was the grand vizier who had failed to keep his boyhood promise.

Making a promise without considering its consequences isn't always fatal, but it can be, as the hero Achilles learned.

Achilles was a minor prince in the north of Greece. His mother, the sea nymph Thetis, spoiled him rotten. She was so protective of her darling mortal son that she took the infant down into the Underworld and, holding him by his heel, dipped him into the river Styx to make his body impervious to human wounds. As a young man Achilles was proud and fierce, renowned throughout Greece as a superb warrior. His pride led him to seek the greatest prize of his age.

King Tyndareus had a problem not many husbands will ever have to deal with but which any father would sympathize with. His wife, a great beauty, had been impregnated by none other than Zeus himself, and the daughter of that union between the beautiful and the divine had grown up to become the most ravishing beauty of all time. Her name was Helen, and merely to glance at her was to fall irredeemably in love. This, the good king recognized, would present a problem for her future mate.

The king therefore summoned together all the kings who sought her hand and made the suitors give a solemn oath that whomever she would pick as her husband would be defended by all the others. Achilles, though only a boy and only a prince, thought he was good enough for Helen, so he attended the meeting and he made the oath. Helen chose Menelaus, king of the Lacedaemonians.

There the story would have ended, but for another prince in

---

*The Order of the Assassins, by the way, continued to cause innumerable problems, but over the years evolved into its own sect—the Ismaili. Today Hassan-i Sabbah's living descendent is known as the Aga Khan, and the present holder of that title occupies the office of U.N. High Commissioner for Refugees.

faraway Troy. The handsome prince Paris was asked by the goddesses Hera, Athena, and Aphrodite to settle a long-standing argument: Who was the fairest among them? While he pondered the matter, each surreptitiously contrived a way to get him alone and offer him a bribe. When the moment for the announcement came, Paris awarded the golden apple to Aphrodite, who had promised him the most beautiful woman in the world as his reward. On receiving the apple, she told him to set sail for Greece.

Warmly welcomed into Menelaus' court, Paris soon spotted Helen, and Aphrodite cast her spell. The two ran off to Troy. Menelaus immediately sent out an alarm to the fellow suitors, who were outraged at the effrontery of a Trojan stealing a bride they had failed to win, and preparations began for an invasion. But as the kings gathered for their war councils, one of Helen's suitors was missing. Achilles was nowhere to be found.

King Odysseus of Ithaca volunteered to travel north to find him. Arriving at the court of Achilles' father, Odysseus was told the young man had gone south to do his duty. In truth, Achilles was desperately trying to avoid his duty and had disguised himself as a woman, pretending to work at spinning with the other women in the great hall of his father's palace. Odysseus was too clever for such a ruse, and, spotting the suspicious character, threw something into Achilles' lap. Achilles let it fall, since the masculine instinct is to separate the knees, whereas any woman would have brought them together. (The same archetypal trick would unmask Tom Sawyer some thirty-one centuries later.) Achilles was soon on a warship headed for Troy.

Achilles' reluctance was wiser than his oath. After ten long years of war, during which he alternately fought with valor or sulked in his tent, the great warrior was slain by Paris when the Trojan got off a lucky shot that struck Achilles in his unprotected heel.

According to *The Odyssey*, Achilles would bemoan the consequences of his promise for all ages to come. When Odysseus went down to the Underworld and encountered the young warrior again, he saluted him as a man "blest by fortune" who was "one of the immortals" and counseled him that he need not be pained by death.

Achilles answered, "Let me hear no more smooth talk of

death from you, Odysseus, light of councils. Better, I say, to break sod as a farmhand for some poor country man on iron rations than to lord it over all of the exhausted dead."

▷ Remember: Achilles professed his oath to Helen's father as if he were ordering up an entrée at a restaurant. If you aren't prepared to make your actions match your words, keep quiet—no matter what the prize. You may lose both the prize and much, much more.

The Counselor Who Castrated Himself

Think for yourself

American soldiers have always been independent thinkers. Washington frequently complained that his troops wouldn't follow an order until they understood the reasons behind it. Civil War commanders often found themselves holding off on attacks until lower-ranking veterans had weighed the pros and cons. No army is a democracy, of course, but this tendency of American soldiers to think for themselves was often credited as an advantage in World War II against the rigid obedience of the Germans and Japanese.

Rigid obedience might be more efficient, but it can lead to disaster. When Lord Lucan ordered the Light Brigade to charge the Russian guns at Balaklava on October 25, 1854, he was on a high hill overlooking the valley. The order was carried down to Lord Cardigan who was observing from a lower plateau. Many historians believe the difference in heights produced a miscommunication. Lucan saw a light artillery emplacement that could easily be taken by the cavalry. Farther down the hill all Cardigan could see was the enemy's well-defended heavy artillery. Cardigan obeyed the order as he understood it, even though it was patently absurd, and ordered his six hundred men to make the famous charge against the entrenched guns. Nearly every soldier in the Light Brigade was killed.

Should Cardigan have disobeyed the order? Of course. Could he have at least questioned it? Certainly. Would he have paid a price? We'll never know. Disobeying orders almost always will carry a price, but if the decision is right it can also bring rich reward. A third-century priest to the Shah of Persia paid the price and reaped the reward.

In 224 A.D. a regional warlord named Ardashir I overthrew and killed the last Parthian king, Artabanus V, and proclaimed himself *Shahahshah,* king of kings. Ardashir then married the king's daughter in order to strengthen his claim to the kingdom.

We do not know the name of Ardashir's new wife, but we do know that four of her brothers survived, two in prison and two who escaped to India. One of the exiled brothers sent by secret means a vial of poison to his sister, with the message to kill their father's usurper. Returning one day from hunting, Ardashir received from his wife a goblet of refreshing liquid into which the poison had been poured. When he accidentally dropped it, his wife became overly distraught. The new shah's suspicions were aroused, and he ordered that some unfortunate domestic fowls be fed the spilled dregs of the cup. They died on the spot. Ardashir then ordered his chief priest to take the princess away immediately and have her ritually executed without delay.

The priest, learning from the princess that she was pregnant, and bearing in mind that Ardashir was childless, decided to disobey the shah and shelter the princess in his own house. Well aware of the danger he was in, that same day he cut off his testicles, and, preserving them in salt, placed them in a casket, which he locked and sealed. He took the casket to the shah and requested that it be placed, unopened, in the treasury with a note attached to it giving the date and the owner's name.

In time, the princess gave birth to a boy "of royal mien and clear spirit," and the priest named him Shapur. Seven years passed, and Ardashir made many conquests, extending the empire and bringing wealth to his people. Meanwhile, the boy grew up, broad-shouldered and possessing the quality of *farr*, the divine spark of kingship. One day, at the court, the priest happened to congratulate the shah on all that he had achieved: "The world in all its seven climes is under your sovereignty; yours are the army, the throne, and the dominion." But Ardashir was under a black cloud of depression:

> My years have reached fifty-one, the musk has turned to camphor and the roses have vanished. I should now have a son standing before me, to comfort my heart, fortify me, and guide me on my path. A father without a son is like an orphaned child who must be taken to the bosom of strangers. After me my throne and crown will pass to an enemy; the dust will be all my profit after my pain and toil.

This was the moment the priest had been waiting for. He had the casket brought from the treasury and the seal broken, and he explained to the shah that he had castrated himself seven years before so that his conduct would now be above suspicion. He then confessed that he had allowed the princess to live and that she had a seven-year-old boy who was the shah's son.

Ardashir was naturally stirred in his heart, but was also suspicious. He wanted proof that this was indeed his son. So he commanded the priest to assemble a hundred boys of the same age, build, and appearance as his alleged son; have them all dressed alike; be given horses, polo mallets, and balls; and then appear on the polo ground, where the shah and his courtiers would attend a polo match at dawn the next day. The game began and, although the boys were some distance from the shah, he saw one boy drive the ball farther than all the rest. Pointing to him, the shah declared to the priest, "There is one of the blood of Ardashir." To confirm his opinion the shah ordered a slave to drive a ball closer to where he was sitting, to where only the boldest of the boys would dare approach.

The shah's slave rode into the midst of the boys and drove a ball in the shah's direction. The boys galloped after it but then reined in before they came too close to the royal presence. Except for "Shapur the Lion," who without hesitation rode up to the shah and retrieved the ball right in front of him. At the sight of the boy, the shah seemed to change before all their eyes from an old to a young man again, so moved was he by the presence of his son, whom he now announced to his nobles as his heir.

Ardashir lavished gold and jewels on the priest and had him placed upon a golden throne, while he commanded that the princess be brought to him, publicly forgiving her and making her once more his consort. To commemorate his newfound happiness, he ordered that a city be founded where before nothing had grown but thorns, symbolizing his change of fortune. Thus, it is said, there came into being the city of Jundi Shapur in Khuzistan.

Following his accession to the throne in 241, Shapur vigorously pursued his father's expansionist policies both in the West, where he defeated the Romans, and in the East, where he seized extensive territories in Central Asia, Afghanistan, and the Kabul valley, stretching to the Indus. But Shapur's place in history rests not only on his imperial vision but also on his vigorous restoration of Zoroastrianism, the ancient religion of the Persians. His fervor may have been a mark of gratitude, for he owed his throne to a priest courageous enough to castrate himself.

▶ Remember: Disobeying orders always entails risk, and may carry a price, but if obedience will lead to failure and disobedience to success, the risk is worth it. Don't let anyone else do your thinking for you.

The Wizard Who Enriched the Vatican

Give your best people room to do their jobs

The Emperor Augustus was once presented with the credentials of a candidate for a secretarial position on his personal staff. "Is he the best man in the empire?" inquired the emperor. "In the entire Roman Empire?" the chamberlain asked with some exasperation. "How could I know?" "Bring me the best man in the empire," said Augustus placidly as he turned to other business.

To search out the best is only the first step. The real secret is in enabling them to do what they do best. The point has never been made better than in a little known but remarkable story about how a modern pope revived the Vatican's fortunes at a desperate time. It begins with a problem Mussolini had created for himself.

Mussolini came to power on an anticlerical, pro-Socialist wave in 1922. To pave the way for his new order he arrested Catholic lay leaders, branded the clergy as traitors, closed churches, forbade Catholic education in the schools, and threatened to take control of Vatican City.

But Mussolini then found himself in a box. His campaign against the Church had not only created a backlash in Italy but also stirred worldwide opposition. He found himself on the way to becoming an international pariah, with a significant opposition building in Italy. To restore his position Mussolini offered a deal to the Vatican.

Although Pius XI loathed the pompous fascist, he too was in a box that Mussolini didn't know about. The Holy See was stone-broke. Its major source of income had vanished with the loss of the Papal States in 1870, and nothing had replaced it. By 1914 Pope Benedict XV had been reduced to hoarding the few gold coins left of the Vatican's treasury in a metal box under his bed. In one year the Archdiocese of Chicago secretly mortgaged all its properties in order to advance $1.5 million to keep the Vatican operating.

With the dictator ignorant of its desperate condition, the

Vatican drove a hard bargain. To reduce tensions with the Church, Mussolini restored Catholic teaching in Italian schools, declared Catholicism once again to be the established religion of Italy, recognized the Holy See as an independent state, and paid restitution for its loss of the Papal States, to the tune of $92.1 million, payable in American dollars.

The cash payment perplexed Pius XI. He knew this money must be made to grow, but he had no idea how such a thing was done. Being from Milan, the financial center of Italy, he could however make inquiries to find someone who did.

In June 1929 the pope gave a personal audience to a young banker by the name of Bernadino Nogara. The banker was respected in Milan as an exceedingly shrewd, if somewhat unorthodox, investment manager. Pius had heard enough to believe that Nogara might be the most brilliant money manager in Italy. The meeting was rare in papal history in that no mention of it exists on the official calendar and no minutes were kept.

The pope turned over to Nogara the entire sum paid by Mussolini. The pope had only one requirement, which was that the papacy would never—ever—be put in such a precarious financial position again. The pope would ask no questions, make no requests, brook no interference. In return, Nogara agreed to dedicate the rest of his life to the task.

Secluded in a small office in the papal apartments, aided only by a clerk and a secretary—both laypeople like himself—Nogara created the Office of Special Administration of the Holy See and began to invest the money paid by Mussolini. By nature a discreet man, in this new position he became secretive in the extreme. He personally prepared a report to the Holy Father only once a year, on a single piece of paper, which he handed directly to the pope. No one else in the Vatican or anywhere else had the slightest idea of what the financier was up to.

But this was, after all, the Vatican, and there were rumors. Nogara was a farsighted man. He saw the new industry of pharmaceuticals being born, and invested heavily. He watched the alliance between *il Duce* and the Führer ripen, and bought stock in munitions companies. Investments in companies that produced birth control pills, or in munitions designed to kill people, served to aggravate the rumors. But the pope held firm to his promise. When Pius XI died in 1939, Pius XII upheld the bargain.

Nogara had prepared well for the Second World War. As Poland and other countries were invaded, and when the Nazis began to harass and then arrest bishops in Germany and elsewhere, he arranged for the secret conversion of diocesan funds into gold and, using Vatican neutrality and contacts on both sides, managed to send large shipments to safe storage in London. When London came under attack in the Blitz and invasion seemed imminent, he somehow persuaded Lord Halifax, Britain's foreign minister, to provide an escort of warships to transport the Vatican's hard assets to the United States.

When the Nazis took direct control of Italy in September 1943, and Hitler threatened the Holy See itself, Nogara managed to slip more gold to the Federal Reserve Bank in New York. Concealed under medical supplies, the bullion moved out of Vatican City right past the German soldiers who ringed it.

Cardinals around the world, with their Vatican-issued international passports, became accustomed to midnight telegrams advising them to pick up a suitcase at a certain place, board a certain flight, and deliver the suitcase to a certain destination. Many of these Princes of the Church were incensed at the idea of being used as messenger boys. Nogara was indifferent to their complaints. The suitcases were stuffed with currencies.

Despite vociferous complaints within the Vatican, the pope threw an iron shield around Nogara's operation. In the postwar period his financial foresight proved itself once again. He formed consortiums with major banking houses to finance the reconstruction of war-torn Europe. Advised by J. P. Morgan & Co. that the United States would enter into a postwar boom, he bought huge parcels of American real estate in what would later be known as suburbia. Noting the shift of population to California, he financed the founding of Bank of America, and for some time the Vatican held fifty-one percent of its stock. He became the single largest investor in the emerging economies of Latin America.

When in the early 1950s Nogara retired (no one is certain of the exact date, because no announcement was made), the Vatican's position was secure beyond the wildest dreams of Pius XI. In 1952 the United Nations' *World Magazine* estimated the Vatican's gold reserves alone were worth several billion and easily greater than those of Britain and France combined. In the United States, the Holy See held major positions in Chase Manhattan Bank, Morgan Guaranty, Bankers Trust, General Motors, General Electric, and Bethlehem Steel, not to mention Bank of America, just as the postwar boom was getting under way. *The Wall Street Journal* in 1955 estimated the Vatican's investments in American stocks, bonds, and real estate conservatively at $80 billion—and that was just one country.

In the early 1950s a special commission of Roman cardinals demanded an investigation into Nogara's investments. In a meeting before the Holy Father, one cardinal rebutted the commission's charges, saying, "Nogara is the best thing to happen to the Vatican since Our Lord Jesus Christ."

There was more than one reason for such a connection to be made. Like the founder of Christianity himself, Bernadino Nogara was a Jew.

▶ **Remember: Hire the best people you can and let them do what you hired them to do. Pius XI didn't care about matters irrelevant to the job he wanted done. He searched for the best, found him, then turned him loose. As it happened, he had found the best money manager in Europe—and perhaps of all time.**

Why Christianity Has a Creed

Stick to your mission until you achieve it

Julius Caesar knew what he wanted. Once in the Alps he and his men came across a miserable little village where they encamped for a few days. His men were amused by the scheming and intrigue of the villagers over the question of who would be the next head man, and they wondered aloud why anyone would want the job. Caesar answered them seriously, "For my part, I would rather be the chief of this village than be the second man in Rome."

Knowing one's destination is half the key to getting there. When Greta Garbo was a young aspiring actress her agent fought to get her a minor part in a movie. He was gleeful when she was given the role, but Garbo turned it down, telling him, "I was born to be a star."

What applies to careers also applies to convictions. Cato the Elder is remembered today for one sentence with which he ended every speech on any subject before the Roman Senate: "*Carthago delenda est!*" or "Carthage must be destroyed!" That one sentence had its effect. In 146 B.C. the Romans destroyed Carthage, and to make sure nothing was left alive, spread salt over its ruins.

No one ever had a clearer sense of mission than a fourth-century bishop who took on his fellow bishops, public opinion, and even his emperors, in defense of orthodox Christianity. Without Athanasius, the Christian religion likely would have degenerated into an earlier version of Islam.

The Prophet Muhammad wrote in the Koran that "God neither begets nor is begotten." This was Islam's answer to the central tenet of Christianity as expressed in the Nicene Creed: that Jesus was no mere prophet or specially favored person but that he is eternally "God from God, Light from Light, True God from True God, begotten not made, one in Being with the Father."

No one knows who actually wrote those lyrical words at the Council of Nicaea in 325, but we do know Athanasius was there. He was to spend the rest of his life passionately committed to their truth.

As soon as the creed was written it was attacked. A Greek theologian by the name of Arius argued that God alone was without beginning, and therefore the Son could not be truly equal to the Father. Jesus may have been exalted by God for doing his will, Arius argued, but he could not be part of the Godhead itself. Jesus should be thought of as a kind of demigod.

When Arius launched his attack Christianity was far from a settled issue, and in fact most people knew very little about it. Even Constantine himself, who had convened the Council in Nicaea, still held to the ancient paganism of his empire. The old ways may have declined in their public practice, but they were still deeply entrenched. Arius's notion of a demigod was familiar; after all, most emperors had become demigods. Arianism began to take hold as a way of understanding this new Christian religion, and soon enough had its backers in the highest reaches of government. Even bishops found themselves using its language and arguments in their teachings and, to one degree or another, coming to accept its basic premises.

Amid this tide of popular and intellectual opinion, Athanasius became bishop of Alexandria, one of the great centers of learning in the ancient world and therefore one of the Church's most prestigious dioceses. Athanasius vowed to stop Arianism—this paganization of the Gospel—in its tracks. He launched broadside after broadside disputing its scriptural moorings and ridiculing its proponents. Stunned and insulted and perhaps a little abashed, Arian sympathizers at court moved to quash him. The emperor, who was no theologian, ordered Athanasius to accept Arius himself as a priest in Alexandria. Not on your life, replied the young bishop. The emperor backed down.

When that didn't work, the Arian supporters decided on a new tactic. They would use the civil courts to remove the recalcitrant bishop from his diocese. First, an accusation of misappropriation was leveled against him. In a trial before the emperor, Athanasius routed his accusers. Next, an accusation of murder was lodged against him. Knowing the supposed victim was alive and in hiding, Athanasius ignored the summons until imperial troops were sent to arrest him. This time the trial was before a court of angry bishops; Athanasius fled to Constantinople, where he appealed to the emperor. Aggravated by this troublesome priest and hoping to calm matters down, Constantine sent him into exile for two years in Germany. The exile was the first of many. Athanasius was thrown out of his diocese five times, and may hold the world's record for being exiled by five different emperors.

His own fellow bishops, trying to please the imperial court while maintaining some grasp on original Christian doctrine, wavered and waffled, and finally—as opposition to him reached a fever pitch—condemned him. Through it all, Athanasius kept at his steady drumbeat, in letters and sermons and published broadsides defending the Nicene Creed as the essential statement of the faith. He thundered, he argued, he reasoned, he ridiculed, and he never let up, day after day.

In the end, Athanasius had one thing going for him that he could not have expected.

The Roman Christians spoke Latin, a practical language with none of the artful subtleties employed by the Arians in their elegant Greek. Fine theological distinctions and imaginative speculations were not the Roman style.

Athanasius found an audience among these Romans, who grew to admire the fiery intellectual from Alexandria. Their admiration mattered, for these sturdy Romans retained a prerogative that even emperors had to acknowledge: they elected the pope.

In 364—after thirty-nine years of battle—the pope in Rome confirmed Athanasius in his teaching and pronounced *anathema* on anyone who disputed the Nicene Creed.

Nine years later Athanasius died.

To this day the Nicene Creed is recited in churches of all denominations in every language every week by nearly two billion Christians.

In the Roman Calendar of the Saints the Alexandrian bishop is listed not only by name but by the title he came to be called during the long struggle sixteen hundred years ago. He is Athanasius *Contra Mundum*, Athanasius "Against the World."

▶ Remember: Athanasius never let up. He knew his mission and he
never allowed anything—edicts, arrests, exile—to keep him from
it. Keep your sights on your objective until you reach it.

The Rothschild Who Bet on Waterloo

Develop your own sources of information

Every workday thousands of analysts in their Wall Street cubicles
pore over hundreds of corporate reports, filings, government sta-
tistics, and market data like ancient augurs trying to discern the
future from the entrails of a chicken. They are searching, of
course, for information.

We live in the so-called age of information, and yet in all its
abundance nothing is scarcer than information that is reliable,
up-to-date, and usable. When the British first broke the German
code with the famous Enigma machine, put together by the country's best mathematicians and chess players, the first thing they
learned was the Luftwaffe's plan to bomb Coventry. If they scram-
bled extra forces to meet the attack, the Germans would be alerted
that the code had been broken. So they watched in frustration as
the town was bombarded into rubble.

Developing sources of information takes time and effort, but
the payoff can be huge. In nineteenth-century England the one
man who knew that better than anyone was Nathan Rothschild.

In 1815 the battle that would change the world was forming
near the small town of Waterloo in Belgium. Napoleon had escaped his exile at Elba, reclaimed his throne, and reignited the
hopes of France. The European alliance had formed against him,
and now the fate of nations hung in the balance. Would Napoleon
bring another decade of conquest and war—or would a conclu-
sive defeat bring him down once and for all?

The London branch of the great Rothschild banking house perhaps had more riding on the battle than anyone but the soldiers who would fight it. Nathan Rothschild as usual exuded absolute calm. This stoic mien had served him well on the London Exchange, where he often appeared personally, leaning against a pillar, to supervise his family's position.

Nathan was the third of five sons of Mayer Rothschild of Frankfurt, the founder of the banking house and the shrewd counselor for all its operations. Mayer's sons were strategically located: Nathan in London, Salomon in Vienna, James in Paris, Kalmann in Milan, and Amschel with his father in Frankfurt.

Through this network the family financed the nobility of Europe, ignoring national boundaries and avoiding the vagaries of war. Their discretion was unimpeachable, their information was flawless, and their reputation for making money for all concerned gave them entrée wherever they chose.

Nathan in London had good reason to take a keen interest in Wellington's battle. He had staked the family fortune on the arming and supply of Wellington's vast army, employing the family network to pass gold from Spain across the Pyrenees and through the heart of France. As a result, he was the largest single holder of British bonds. The outcome of Waterloo would determine the fate of the House of Rothschild.

The Rothschilds for years had invested in maintaining a vast network of informants, augmented by their own private messenger service. Day and night Rothschild coaches sped along Europe's highways, and Rothschild ships set fast sail across the Channel. The blue uniform of the Rothschild couriers was as well known to nineteenth-century Europe as the uniforms of the various national armies. These messengers carried securities, debt instruments, orders to buy and sell, but most of all they carried news—news of harvests, news of weather, news of royal alliances—news that moved markets.

No news was more important than the outcome of the battle of Waterloo. The great clash occurred on June 18, 1815. Word that Wellington had committed his troops was sent to London as soon as the battle commenced. On the morning of the nineteenth, Nathan slipped out of town and made his way to Folkestone harbor. That same morning on the other side of the Channel, a Rothschild agent by the name of Rothworth grabbed the first edition of a Dutch gazette that confirmed what he had already learned. He then ran to a waiting Rothschild boat. A few hours later he put the paper in Nathan's hands. Nathan scanned the headline, jumped in his coach, and sped to London. He stopped first at Whitehall to inform the government of its great victory, then made his way quickly to the Exchange.

He entered the Exchange as if he had walked from his home and coolly took up his familiar position, leaning against a pillar. He motioned to his brokers. The Exchange became quiet. The Rothschild reputation for inside information was well established, and on this day nobody was going to bet against it. The Rothschild brokers began to sell British bonds. That could only mean one thing: Wellington's defeat. The price began to fall. Nathan continued to sell, and to sell even more, still leaning expressionless against his pillar. The price collapsed.

Then Nathan bought. He bought every British bond on the market, hundreds of thousands of pounds' worth of bonds, for a song. Moments after the buy order was executed the great news broke that Wellington had won.

On one day, by one action, a profitable family merchant bank was transformed into one of the world's great fortunes. Sixty years later the Rothschilds would, at the behest of Benjamin Disraeli, finance the building of the Suez Canal when England didn't have the funds. Seventy years after that they would participate in financing the reconstruction of postwar Europe.

As Rothschild biographer Frederic Morton put it, "We cannot estimate how many liveried servants, how many Watteaus and Rembrandts, how many thoroughbreds in his descendants' stables, the man by the pillar won that single day."

▶ **Remember: Rothschild didn't make his family's fortune by relying on others for his information. His sources were established, ready to act, and reliable. And Rothschild knew how to capitalize on what they brought him.**

The Athenian Who Built Ships Out of Silver

Prepare for tomorrow

"When the savages of Louisiana are desirous of fruit," wrote Montesquieu, "they cut down the tree to the root, and gather the fruit." Judging by the less-than-robust state of its economy, the savages may still run loose in Louisiana. In his famous *Gallic Wars* Caesar recounts instances of whole tribes on the move whose chieftains had taken no precautions to provide for them, thinking the land would suffice. When a harsh winter occurred the same year as their migration, the land had nothing to give. The tribes suffered terribly, and became easy marks for other tribes with more prescient leaders.

Sudden wealth seems to produce the same impulse as sudden need. A newly acquired mistress of Louis XV began to throw lavish parties and bestow jewels on all her friends. "Little girl," admonished a sympathetic noble, "don't you understand that the same king who admires your dimple today will discover a wart tomorrow?"

The twin tempters of any society are sudden need and sudden wealth. How its leaders respond in either case will determine that society's—nation's, company's, organization's, family's—survival.

For Athens in the fifth century B.C. the test came in the form of a major new vein discovered in a silver mine.

By 482 the mine at Laurium was producing such prodigious amounts of silver from its newly discovered vein that the Athenian assembly met to consider what to do with the city's phenomenal new wealth. A proposal was immediately put forward to distribute the unexpected treasure among the citizens. After all, Athens had no debt, and its current taxes were adequate to its needs. Thrilled at the prospect, the assembly rallied to the idea, and it was quickly endorsed by the archon Aristides—not surprising, considering that the archon in Athens was an elected position, and Aristides was up for re-election.

But a young member of the assembly named Themistocles

stood to oppose the idea. Themistocles argued cogently that to disburse this newfound wealth would be to dissipate it. Athens would never be anything but a second-class city until it invested the money necessary to dredge and enlarge its small harbor at Piraeus and thereby transform itself into a maritime power.

Even at that moment, the young Athenian warned, Xerxes of Persia was known to be gathering shipbuilders and materials from all over his vast empire. For what other purpose than to attack Athens by sea? The silver, Themistocles exclaimed, was sent by the gods who loved and wanted to protect Athens. The new wealth could purchase materials, employ carpenters, and pay to train their men in seamanship.

The speech was a tour de force, and to the archon Aristides' dismay, the assembly reversed itself and committed the newfound money to the dredging of the harbor and the building of a fleet. (It then exiled Aristides for his shortsightedness in not thinking of this earlier.)

Only two years later the Athenians' investment paid off. When word came that Xerxes had gathered together a huge fleet, a delegation was hastily dispatched to the oracle at Delphi to ask what these preparations meant. The answer, as reported by Herodotus, was elliptic at best:

> Wide-seeing Zeus grants to Athena, Triton-born, that
> The wooden wall alone remain unsacked . . .
> O divine Salamis! You shall destroy the children of women . . .

The puzzled Athenians were alarmed. What wooden wall? What did the small island of Salamis have to do with anything? And whose children would be destroyed? Themistocles argued the wooden wall meant Athenian ships, and that the oracle was telling the Athenians to meet the Persian fleet at Salamis.

When Xerxes did indeed attack, his greatest force came by sea. The Athenians were waiting with two hundred new warships. With Themistocles as its admiral, the combined Greek fleet destroyed the Persians at the Battle of Salamis, in what naval historians still regard as one of the ten greatest sea battles ever fought.

The Circus Girl Who Saved an Empire

Go on the offense

Keep your head "while all about you are losing theirs, and blaming it on you," advised Rudyard Kipling. Easier said than done. "My firm nerves shall never tremble," declared Macbeth, but of course that was before he saw "Great Birnam wood to high Dunsinane hill" coming against him, fulfilling the witches' prophecy of how he would be killed.

One evening in July 1830 an excited young nobleman burst into the private rooms of Talleyrand, the wily old diplomat who had survived the French Revolution and Napoleon to represent France at the Congress of Vienna fifteen years before. "Revolutionaries are moving against the palace!" the aide reported breathlessly. Outside, shouts and gunfire could be heard in the distance. "Do not fear," said the old man. "We shall win." "But who is *we*, my prince?" the aide asked with a worried look. The old man glanced at the window, in the direction of the growing tumult. "*That* I shall tell you tomorrow," replied Talleyrand.

Not everyone can play the game as coolly as Talleyrand. Even the most experienced leader can find himself caught up in the panic of others. "I will not budge," said the sheriff when a deputy told him a lynch mob was marching toward the jail to hang his prisoner. "What are they going to do, shoot me?" "That's what they said, Sheriff. Said they were going to shoot you." "Then let's get the hell out of here!"

The Byzantine emperor Justinian I was perhaps the best trained of any who donned the imperial toga. Raised by his uncle, the emperor Justin, he came to power as his uncle's deputy, actually ruling as his apprentice for several years before stepping up to the throne himself. When he died in 565 A.D. Justinian had ruled that vast state for nearly forty years. More than most rulers in world history, an extraordinary number of monuments to his reign have survived. Among them is the architectural wonder of Hagia Sophia, the Church of Holy Wisdom, built in only six years by Justinian as the patriarchal see of Constantinople. More important was his codification of a thousand years of Roman law, an immense undertaking that serves today as the jurisprudential base of legal systems throughout the world, including Japan, continental Europe, South America, and much of Africa.

None of these great achievements would have occurred if Justinian had not married a circus girl.

Theodora was a child of the streets, the daughter of two circus performers. Custom and the law regarded actresses and performers as little better than prostitutes, which seems not to have bothered Theodora a bit. One story tells of a famous dance she performed at the Hippodrome with an aged male lion, and without too much in the way of clothes. She was wild, no doubt about it, and enjoyed many lovers—until the day she was introduced to Justinian.

Theodora was twenty-three, and Justinian was forty-four. The electricity between them was instant, total, and lasted for both of their lifetimes. Head over heels in love, Justinian persuaded his uncle the emperor to repeal the venerable law prohibiting men of senatorial rank from marrying actresses. (Later in his *Code* he made the revision permanent, and thereby opened the door to marriage for many lovers of disparate station.)

In 527 the two lovers were crowned jointly as emperor and

empress of the Roman Empire. Five years later, Justinian was to have cause to be glad of his taste in women. Beautiful and trained to please, Theodora also proved to have nerves of steel.

The Byzantine capital was always a seething cauldron of intrigue and conspiracy, but in 532 discontent over Justinian's taxes was seized on by factions opposed to him as a cause for actual insurrection. The rebellion precipitated a full-scale riot, and soon Constantinople was in flames. The rebels used the confusion to launch an attack on the palace.

Justinian was shaken to his core. A ship was ordered to stand by to carry the royal couple into exile, as with so many emperors before and after. Justinian ordered Theodora to grab whatever she could; their only choice was to flee. Theodora stood her ground. She told Justinian to go without her. "For me," she said, "majesty is the best winding sheet." The circus girl would rather die than surrender the throne she had gained.

Stiffened in his resolve by the determination of his wife, Justinian hurriedly organized the Huns who made up his imperial bodyguard, and then ordered them out into the streets, where rebels and rioters alike were slaughtered. The ferocity of Justinian's attack sent the insurrectionists running for their lives. The empire—and Theodora's throne—were saved.

The two would reign together for twenty-one years until Theodora's death. For another seventeen years after that Justinian carried on alone.

▶ **Remember: Panic leads to paralysis. Situations will sometimes fly out of control. The moment of greatest danger is often the best moment to strike. Theodora was willing to risk her life to keep her throne. In that she reminded Justinian of what it means to be an emperor.**

How Washington Stopped a Coup

Confront a bad situation head-on

The image we hold of George Washington as an aloof Olympian figure does an injustice to the man's personality. Among friends and family he was warm, considerate, and even playful. His Sunday dinners at Mount Vernon were famous for their good food, liberally poured wine, and ribald stories.

But on the job Washington was magisterial. A roomful of officers were once celebrating a breakthrough in the long Revolutionary War when Alexander Hamilton, carried away by the good feeling, put his hand on the general's shoulder. The room instantly froze. Washington turned and walked from the room.

The secret of leadership is distance, and Washington knew it. Napoleon was said to have commanded with his eyes. Washington commanded with his implacable reserve. His men did not fear him, and they did not love him. They held him in awe.

Pulitzer Prize–winning historian James Thomas Flexner called him "the indispensable man," arguing that he was among only a handful of figures who forever altered the course of history. Without him the United States would not have been born—and without him it most certainly would not have survived.

Not many Americans realize that a military coup nearly toppled the United States before it got started. How it was stopped boils down to a single confrontation in Newburgh, New York, in the early spring of 1783.

Two years before, Cornwallis had surrendered to Washington at Yorktown. As the peace negotiations in Versailles dragged on, Washington kept his army encamped at a strategic location on the Hudson River. It was not a happy place. The war had wreaked havoc on the fledgling country's economy. While the politicians bickered over the form the new government was to take, the army remained poorly paid, and the officer corps was often not paid at all. Meanwhile, many of their farms had been ruined and their families turned out to depend on the charity of neighbors. Not surprising, the army's camp was seething with discontent.

Some states reluctantly paid a portion of their tax revenues to the national government, while others refused to pay anything. Congress only controlled duties from imports, and with a destroyed economy there was not enough ready cash to import much worth taxing.

The officer corps saw the political problem clearly. Nothing would be resolved under the existing loose Confederation. What was needed was a strong national government that could impose taxation, clear the nation's debts, restore its credit, and if necessary defend its hard-fought-for freedom against the great powers that surrounded its territory on all sides—Britain to the north, Spain to the south, and France to the west.

At first the officers and many of their fellow countrymen had put their hope in the idea that Washington would allow himself to be proclaimed king. Every other nation was ruled along monarchical lines; it was the only form of government people knew and understood. But Washington's adamance on the subject was well known, and an adamant Washington was not someone who would be swayed.

The officers then began to explore the idea of a temporary military regime that would seize the reins of government, establish financial discipline, and after two years or so step down in favor of civilian elections. Letters began circulating among the encamped officers in Newburgh and then to fellow officers in the most important states. The plan called for military forces on the same day to seize not only the national capital at Philadelphia, but also the key cities of Boston, New York, and Richmond. A "government of national union" would be proclaimed. With the army in control, resistance would be easily crushed, although the officers doubted many sensible men would oppose such a rational solution to the nation's evident woes. A meeting held in Newburgh on March 7, 1783, confirmed the plan's particulars.

Washington knew nothing about it. Nobody doubted that he would oppose any hint of sedition. But once the coup had taken place and matters were irrevocably set, his men reasoned, the general would have no alternative but to take control of the nation.

But this was still Washington's camp, and this was still his

army. One of his aides could no longer bear the burden of disloy-
alty by keeping the general in the dark. He broke down and told
the general of the plot. Washington was appalled—but he faced a
dilemma. If he merely ordered the plotters to halt their scheme, he
probably would be ignored, and his authority over the army
would be permanently weakened. On the other hand, if he did
nothing, his officers would surely succeed, and the great democratic experiment he had labored to launch would be dead before
it was born. The only avenue open to him was to meet with his
men and try to dissuade them from their course. He summoned
the officer corps.

The officers knew what this was about, and they were prepared for it. Before the meeting started they unanimously resolved
not to be moved by anything Washington said, to give him the respect he was due, but to move forward resolutely with the plan.

When Washington entered the room and walked to the
podium, the officers rose as one. Washington immediately sensed
their determination in the impassiveness of their faces. They
stared straight ahead. Washington began to speak. He told them of
his love for them, and reminded them of all they had accomplished together. He assured them that their just complaints
would be heard "despite the slowness inherent in deliberative
bodies." He urged them not "to open the floodgates of civil dis-
cord, and deluge our rising empire in blood."

At the end of his speech, Washington looked out on his men,
and saw that he had failed to budge them. Desperate, reaching for
any straw that might divert the disaster, he remembered a letter
from a congressman he had recently received that indicated all
would soon be settled in the army's favor. As he fumbled for it in
his pocket, he pulled out another piece of paper but not the letter.
He appeared momentarily confused, which was shocking to his
audience, who had never seen Washington at a loss for anything
during seven long years of war. Then the general reached into another pocket for his eyeglasses.

"Gentlemen," he said, "you will permit me to put on my spec-
tacles, for it seems I have not only grown gray but almost blind in
the service of my country."

Washington looked up to see tears in the eyes of his men. Tears began to well in his own. That could not be allowed. He stiffened and strode from the room.

He left behind an audience of hardened soldiers with tears running down their cheeks. The coup was dead.

▶ Remember: Washington didn't blame his men, he didn't denounce them, he didn't issue an order, nor threaten to arrest them. But he did confront them. As an experienced warrior, he knew full well the consequences of inaction at a moment of peril. Never ignore a bad situation. Don't overreact to it, but do step up to it.

The Kamikaze That Saved Japan

When fortune is in your favor, make the most of it

Can there be a lesson in the weather? "Everybody talks about the weather," said Mark Twain, "but nobody does anything about it." Yet Montesquieu argued that climate and geography shape human culture. Weather makes the Swedes suicidal, the Germans organized, the Scots dour, the Mediterranean peoples carefree, and the tropical peoples torpid. Heat caused the Southern drawl, and New England winters instilled Yankee reserve.

A wrong prediction on the weather can have disastrous results. The Spanish Armada was pounded to pieces in July 1588—an especially tempestuous season in the English Channel. Napoleon's humiliating retreat from wintry Moscow in 1812 wreaked such misery on his troops that he never recovered. And in 1281 a hurricane hit the shores of Japan at such a propitious moment that it entered into the nation's mythology and shaped the national character for hundreds of years to follow.

For more than six hundred years the great dynasties of China—the Sui, the T'ang, and the Sung—had achieved such power and wealth that they had created the largest and most firmly governed nation on earth. Every nation surrounding it was expected to bow to its suzerainty, and its literature, culture, religious movements, and philosophy permeated the Eastern world. Japan was also deeply influenced by China, but it was too isolated and too proud of its own identity to become a vassal state.

When an early empress of Japan replied to a diplomatic overture from the Chinese court by saluting "the land of the setting sun from the land of the rising sun," the insult was considered so profound that a war might have ensued but for the quick work—and adroit bribery—of the Japanese ambassador in Beijing, who undoubtedly saved his own life in the bargain.

The Mongols who invaded China in 1230 were not so easily assuaged, nor were they interested in the tribute Japan would occasionally render to the imperial court. Kublai Khan ascended to the Mongol throne with the intention of ruling the world.

The great khan's knowledge of Japan appears to have been spotty. He did not seem to know that six hundred years of incessant internecine wars had developed in Japan a strong warrior caste whose code of honor was deeply imbedded. A first invasion force in 1274 consisted of only six thousand or so Mongol and Chinese troops. The Japanese samurai easily rebuffed it in only two days of fighting. But Kublai Khan learned from his mistakes.

After seven years of preparation, which included replanting miles of Korean land to provide harvests of rice for the Mongol troops, a great armada was gathered in 1281 to subdue Japan. It consisted of more than nine hundred ships, fifteen thousand Korean seamen, forty thousand Mongols, and one hundred thousand Chinese troops.

The Japanese had watched the khan's preparations in Korea with mounting alarm. The emperor with great solemnity made processions to the nation's famous shrines to pray for deliverance. Fields went untended as every able warrior was called to the western provinces. The entire military strength of the nation was put into constructing a defensive wall to rebuff the invasion.

The khan had learned to respect Japanese fighting prowess, but he knew his troops were battle-tested. Years of conquest had strengthened their generalship and use of tactics. Meanwhile, on the Japanese side, fifty years of peace had brought prosperity to the land, but prosperity had also dulled the once-hard edge of the nation's military discipline.

The Mongol forces landed at several points along the western coast on June 23, 1281, seizing an important peninsula that could allow them to outflank the Japanese defenders. Only furious and constant assaults prevented the Mongols from dividing the defensive forces and breaching the line. For seven deadly weeks the fighting was fierce as both sides struggled for advantage.

By the second week of August the defenders were exhausted. Japan had thrown every resource at its command into the battle; no reserves were left. Meanwhile, ships constantly scurried back and forth from the Korean ports, bringing fresh troops and supplies to the enemy. Mongol forces would break through the defenses at key points, and the Japanese would valiantly rise to repel them, then collapse at their battle stations as the invaders fell back. The entire nation prayed for a miracle.

On August 15 an immense hurricane arose from the southwest. The Korean shipmasters who saw signs of the storm immediately cast off with whatever troops they had on board. But most ships of the huge fleet were hit with the full force of the storm as it raged toward shore. The number of lost lives has never been accurately calculated, but historians believe that as many as fifty thousand of the invasion force died on the first day. On the second day, the remaining forces on land, stranded and under siege from the elements, were attacked all along the battle line as the Japanese rallied to finish what the gods had started. Thousands were killed, and many more taken prisoner.

Victory was total. Not for seven hundred years, until World War II, would Japan face the threat of invasion again.

The mark of this great storm on the Japanese character is inexpressible. The intervention of the gods confirmed the divine destiny of the Japanese nation. No act of nature has done more to form a people, and no one word has marked its character more than "divine wind"—the *kamikaze.*

▶ **Remember: On the second day of the kamikaze the exhausted Japanese instinctively attacked into the face of the hurricane at every point along a two hundred mile line. Fortune is blind. When it comes your way, don't hesitate to take advantage of it.**

How William Became the Conqueror

Once committed, stay committed

Nobody ever has all the information they need to make a decision. That's because nobody can read tomorrow's newspaper. A decision is necessarily a choice between imponderables. Decision-making comes down to risk assessment: How much will it cost? What can go wrong? What is the payoff? What are the chances? Management theorists have even created a "decision tree" to systematize the process by listing all the possible outcomes and assigning a percentage value to the likelihood of each. The problem, of course, is in assigning the percentages. If you knew for certain you had a ten percent chance of winning a million dollars on a five-dollar bet, you'd make the bet. But how do you know for certain your chance is ten percent and not .000000000000001 percent? The odds are what make decisions so hard. But you have to admire the theorists for trying.

The two most risk-laden decisions in the history of the English-speaking peoples were made eight hundred years apart by two great men looking out at the same water and watching the same sky.

When Edward the Confessor died in 1066 three men disputed the crown of England. Duke William of Normandy claimed his cousin Edward had designated him as heir years before. Harold, earl of Wessex and Edward's brother-in-law, claimed that Edward on his deathbed had designated *him* as heir. Harald of Norway ("the last Viking") claimed it belonged to him by right of descent from his kinsman King Canute.

In September, Harald the Viking struck first on the coast near York, and he was soundly beaten by the lightning-swift attack of Harold the earl, who by now had had himself proclaimed King Harold II of England.

Meanwhile, on the coast of Normandy, the other rival claimant had a terrible decision to make. In the preceding months William had assembled an invasion fleet of seven hundred ships, large and small, seven thousand men, and more than one thousand war horses. For days he had watched a terrible storm whip up the English Channel, one of the nastiest bodies of water in the world. A partial clearing had occurred, but not a complete one. If William's armada set sail and the weather improved, all would be well. But what if the weather got worse?

His men were no Vikings. They were landlubbers; even the crews on his ships were Norman farmboys. And then there were his precious war horses. Horses can't afford to get seasick—they will die rather than vomit. A sudden storm could sicken his men, kill his horses, and scatter his fleet all along the English coast, rendering them unable to regroup and easy pickings for Harold.

That is, if Harold won in the north. William had no way of knowing whether he had, or whether a battle had even been fought. If Harold hadn't won, William would face an even more dangerous enemy: a Norse fleet full of victorious, blood-lusty Vikings sailing south to intercept his ungainly Norman flotilla.

Then again, if William delayed, one of his two enemies could be entrenched and waiting for him when he finally did commit. His men would be slaughtered on the beaches.

William saw the break in the weather was about as much luck as he was going to get. Any delay was a wager based on hope, and hopes flitter away more quickly than dreams. William had dreamed of England since he was a boy, and he meant to have it. On September 27 he gave the order to set sail.

Halfway across the Channel another storm blew in, tossing the Norman ships about like so many pieces of driftwood. As if that was not enough, the storm brought in a thick blanket of fog. The Norman fleet began to break up as the ships lost sight of one another. William's men had been frightened enough by the idea of getting on boats; now they were terrified. Their leader had to do something, but what could anyone do about the weather?

His commanders demanded that the ships head back to safety. William instead ordered a banquet set up on his main deck and told them to sit down and eat up. As Norman vessels scudded past through the shifting fog, the men aboard were amazed to see the duke and his colleagues feasting and toasting to their "adventure." Many a Norman commander must have rushed to the railing that night, but the effect of their duke's show of confidence on the troops was worth a little secret seasickness. There's a storm? No problem.

Upon landing, a disaster worse than the weather happened. As the flagship came in to shore at Pevensey, the duke leapt into the waves and waded ashore. A large wave came crashing in, knocking him down. When it passed over, William found his helmet had been turned around, with its eye holes and noseguard at the back of his head, blinding him completely. Embarrassing, of course, but worse than that—this was a seriously bad omen in an age that believed intensely in omens. (Signs and portents are still the stuff of much discussion among soldiers and sailors.)

Knowing his mission at that moment would succeed or fail by what he did, William stood up and took off the helmet. Holding it high so that his men in the ships could see, he cried out in a loud voice something like, *"Je change mon chef: je viens un duc, je reste un roi!"* or "I'm changing my headpiece: I came here a duke, I'll stay as a king!" Their leader's bon mot was met with cheers from his men. They had seen how he dealt with the forces of nature. Why expect him to be undone by a matter of mere luck?

William found himself on a nearly undefended coast, along which his army easily reassembled and began a leisurely march toward Canterbury. Meanwhile, Harold was forcing his battle-weary troops on double time southward to meet the Norman

low him to appear at court. Finally the king forgave Absalom and allowed him to retake his public place.

During his years out of the limelight, Absalom had been plotting. As soon as he received the king's blessing, he bought a chariot and horses and hired fifty men to act as a royal retinue. He looked every inch the prince. As the biblical chronicler tells us, "In all Israel there was no one more praised as Absalom for his beauty: from the sole of his foot even to the crown of his head, there was no blemish on him. When he polled his head (for it was at every year's end that he polled it: because the hair was heavy on him, therefore he polled it), he weighed the hair of his head at two hundred shekels, after the king's weight." (II Samuel 14:15–26)

Early every morning Absalom paraded through the streets of Jerusalem to the city gates. There he would station himself to receive petitioners on their way to the royal courts. If they were from the northern tribes, he would pointedly question the justice they received from the southern judges appointed by his father. For four years he courted the favor of the northern Israelites, and by playing on the political divisions of the kingdom he became popular among the larger tribes.

Now Absalom felt the moment was at hand. Absalom asked for David's permission to make a religious pilgrimage to the city of Hebron, David's old capital of Judah in the days before he united the kingdom. There Absalom raised his standard, declaring the time had come for the northern tribes of Israel to reclaim the kingdom. Because he was the first to declare himself, thousands of the disaffected flocked to him, including such important men as Ahithophel, renowned as David's counselor.

The king was older now, but hardly infirm. He may not have possessed the same strength of arm that killed Goliath, but he had lost none of his decisiveness and cunning. The minute the messenger arrived in Jerusalem shouting the alarm, David ordered his guards to pack up and flee. In the dead of night he and his loyalists set out on foot, hoping to make their way across the desert to safety before Absalom could catch up with them.

Among those in the city who rushed to join the king in his escape was Hushai, a longtime friend. But David wouldn't let him go, fearing for his friend's old age. Instead he told Hushai to welcome Absalom to Jerusalem and pledge support to him, then to use his position to confound the good counsel that would surely be given by Ahithophel. Hushai reluctantly agreed to stay, then bade farewell as the king and his men moved out into the night.

The next morning Absalom entered Jerusalem in triumph. The first order of business was to locate and destroy the loyalist band that had escaped. Ahithophel counseled immediate action, for if the king were not found and killed, he could rally the nation around him. Hushai counseled caution, "For all Israel knoweth that thy father is a mighty man, and they which be with him are valiant men" (II Samuel 17:10). If Absalom attacked now, Hushai advised, many men would be lost, and the rest would be disheartened. Better to wait until more warriors could be enlisted, and then crush David and his men with one blow.

Absalom sided with Hushai. Ahithophel, who knew David well, understood what this meant. "When Ahithophel saw that his advice had not been followed," the chronicler tells us, "he saddled his ass and arose, and got him home to his house, to his city, and put his household in order, and hanged himself." (II Samuel 17:23).

The common people in the rural areas rallied to David. By the time Absalom had gathered his forces and crossed the Jordan to seek out his father, he was met with a formidable army under David's experienced commanders. David issued one instruction: "No harm to Absalom."

During the battle Absalom encountered a loyalist vanguard. Turning his horse to retreat, his extravagant hair became entangled in some oak branches. The horse moved on, leaving him hanging. The troops immediately sent word to Joab, one of David's generals, who came to see for himself. Over the protest of the troops, who were well aware of the king's orders, Joab pulled out three javelins and threw them into Absalom's heart. He then sent his personal guards to finish off the prince.

When David was told of Absalom's death, he covered his face and cried aloud, "Absalom, O Absalom. If only I had died instead of you!"

But that cry came from David the father. David the king ruled Israel, and it was David the king who had acted to save his throne. Knowing that his son's innate caution could be played against him, David the king had skillfully exploited it, even as David the father mourned the result.

▶ Remember: David's quick action beat Absalom's caution. Before you decide to act, make sure you have the forces to win. Then strike quickly. In moments of crisis, delay doubles danger.

The Defender, the Assassin, and the Swimmer

Retain the boldness of youth

When Thomas Arnold became headmaster of Rugby School in 1828 at the very young age of thirty-three, he was faced with the task of selecting a new department head. He ignored seniority and chose a tutor who was even younger than himself for the job. A disgruntled teacher complained that his twenty years of experience had been overlooked. "You don't have twenty years experience," said Arnold, who was bent on improving the school's standards. "You have had one year's experience twenty times."

The passed-over teacher may have had a point in his complaint, but Arnold had a better one. Gray hair doesn't signify anything more than that the hair is gray. As the Roman playwright Plautus put it, maturity tells nothing about ability.

The great advantage of youth is its daring. Age ponders while youth acts. And so youth is considered reckless, and age is considered prudent. But as the Romans discovered in the founding of their Republic, in times of distress it is youth's audacity and not age's precaution that will win the day.

In 509 B.C. the patrician families overthrew Rome's king, Tarquin the Proud, an Etruscan of royal blood. This revolutionary act produced a fierce reaction from Tarquin's fellow monarchs in central Italy. Rallied by Lars Porsena, king of Clusium, the Etruscans raised a great army, surrounded Rome, and blockaded it, intending to starve the rebellious inhabitants into submission. Porsena would probably have achieved his end—his blockade was so effective—had not the bravery of three Roman youths steeled the city's determination to win its independence at all costs.

Porsena let his blockade have its desired effect, then looked for a way to penetrate the city's defenses so that his troops could go in for the kill. The weakest point was a wooden bridge across the Tiber that connected the city proper with a sparsely settled suburb on the Janiculum hill. All had been quiet as the Etruscans waited for starvation to do its work, when Porsena launched a sudden attack on Janiculum and sent his troops streaming down the hill toward the bridge. The Roman cohort guarding the bridge was shocked by this sudden onslaught; most threw down their shields and fled to safety on the other side. Only three Roman youths held their ground, among them Horatius Cocles. He ordered his companions to muster the troops and destroy the bridge by whatever means. As the historian Livy recounts the tale, "Proudly he took his stand at the outer end of the bridge; conspicuous amongst the rout of fugitives, sword and shield ready for action, he prepared himself for close combat, one man against an army."

The enemy stood back, stunned by Horatius' preposterous courage. While they hesitated, he strode back and forth shouting insults at the enemy. Finally the Etruscans attacked, and their sheer numbers would have swept the lone defender aside if at that moment a loud crash had not signaled the collapse of the bridge. Horatius leapt into the water fully armed and swam to safety on the other side as the enemy gaped in bewilderment.

With this single avenue of attack closed down, Porsena settled in for a long siege. Rome had water but little food, and conditions inside the city worsened daily. A young patrician named Gaius Mucius grew despondent, not so much at the danger of the situation but at the shame of it. His elders talked and debated; some argued for buying Porsena off with tribute, others that this republican idea was crazy to begin with. How could proud Rome, Mucius wondered, even consider backing down in the face of an enemy it held in contempt?

Mucius determined to take matters into his own hands. He would demoralize the enemy by assassinating Porsena. Without revealing his true intentions, Mucius somehow got permission from the Senate to leave the city. Entering the enemy camp, he maneuvered his way through the crowd close to the raised platform where the king and his secretary were sitting. On this day the king and the secretary happened to be dressed the same, and as most of the men addressed the secretary, Mucius couldn't be sure which one was which. He took a calculated chance and rushed the secretary, stabbing him with a dagger. The deed done, and with cries of alarm all about him, he tried to force his way back through the crowd, but was quickly seized and hauled before the outraged king.

Mucius proudly told the king he had meant to kill him and that others waited in the wings to try again. He expected to die, he said, for "it is our Roman way to do and suffer bravely." Alarmed, Porsena pointed to a fire kindled for a sacrifice and told the young man he would be burned alive if he didn't reveal the details of the assassination plots. Mucius cried, "See how little men care for their bodies when they care only for honor!" and thrust his right hand in the fire. The astonished king ordered him dragged away from the altar and set free to return to Rome.

Shaken by the young man's courage and by the threat of more assassins, Porsena made overtures to the Roman Senate about lifting the siege. To show good faith the two sides exchanged hostages. As the negotiations dragged on (as peace negotiations have ever since), hope for a lasting truce began to fall. Perhaps fearful that the hostages might be taken back to Etruria rather than released, one young female hostage decided to make a break for it. Cloelia organized a few of her companions one day and broke out of their polite confinement, plunged into the Tiber, and started swimming furiously to the Roman side. The Etruscan guards fired volley after volley of arrows, while the Romans on the other side cheered the young women on until they reached safety.

This break of good faith infuriated Porsena, and he made it clear that if Cloelia, at least, did not return, the truce would be ended. Like the good Roman she was, Cloelia bravely gave herself back up to the enemy. Porsena was so impressed by her exploit, as well as by her willingness to return, that he offered to let her choose hostages to be set free. She chose the young men, since they were the most likely to receive the brunt of Etruscan anger. This, too, impressed Porsena, and the negotiations were resumed. Finally the siege was lifted.

Could the Etruscans have won their siege against upstart Rome, and nipped its fledgling Republic in the bud? Perhaps. But Lars Porsena certainly came to believe his effort was futile. The courage of three daring young people taught him that these stiff-necked Romans would never bend.

▶ Remember: Retain the daring of your youth. In moments of crisis or danger, it is daring that wins the day.

The Patron Who Snubbed the Poet

When necessary, make amends quickly

Early in his career Voltaire was thrown into prison by officials upset by his satire of the regent, the Duc d'Orléans. When he was released, Voltaire immediately sent a note to the regent thanking him for his freedom. The regent, embarrassed and well aware of the power of Voltaire's pen, replied promptly, apologizing for the incident and offering a stipend. Voltaire in turn replied, thanking the regent for his concern about his livelihood but advising that "in the future you need not worry yourself about my lodging."

The regent was wise to act quickly. The apology is an art form in itself, and its most important part is timing. An apology delivered too late may follow you into the history books, as one of Islam's most revered heroes discovered.

Mahmud of Ghazni was the first great Muslim sultan who in the eleventh century founded an empire that included Afghanistan, Pakistan, and Persia. Plundering a subcontinent made Mahmud an extremely rich ruler. Thousands of slaves, war elephants, masses of gold and silver, and all sorts of treasures were brought back to his capital of Ghazni. Naturally, artists and writers flocked to his court, and Mahmud's patronage was so generous that he could be regarded as a Medici of the Orient.

In time, the great poet Firdawsi (a pen name meaning "of paradise") arrived at Mahmud's court. He was finishing his epic poem *Shahnama,* or *Book of Kings,* which traces Persian history from the invention of fire to the exploits and upheavals of powerful dynasties by using folklore, fact, and legend. The work had consumed many years of his life, and it was to become Persia's literary masterpiece, eventually elevating Firdawsi to the status of a Homer or a Virgil in Persian eyes.

In return for Firdawsi's completing the *Shahnama* and dedicating it to Mahmud, the sultan had promised to pay the poet fifty thousand dirhams (silver coins). But when the poet presented the finished work, Mahmud harshly criticized it. Perhaps his mind had been poisoned by Firdawsi's rivals at court or perhaps, as a Turk, he did not appreciate an epic (considerably longer than *The Iliad* and *The Odyssey*) that glorified Persian history and culture. He paid Firdawsi an insulting twenty thousand dirhams. The poet was mortified.

Firdawsi went from the palace to the local bathhouse, where he very publicly dispensed half the sum as a tip to the attendant and the other half to a sherbet seller.

His insult having been delivered in return for the insult Mahmud had given him, Firdawsi then fled from Ghazni and sought refuge with a prince of the ancient Persian line. While enjoying the prince's hospitality, Firdawsi penned a vitriolic satire that questioned Mahmud's ancestry and honor.

Firdawsi's protector was a prudent man, and he knew the long arm of the sultan could still reach the offending poet and a petty princeling like himself. He also hoped that, by writing the satire, Firdawsi's spleen against the sultan had been vented.

Still, the prince felt the poet had been wronged by the sultan and was due some compensation. He offered Firdawsi one hundred thousand dirhams—one thousand dirhams for each line of the satire—if he could keep the work for his private pleasure. The next day, Firdawsi received the money and handed over the manuscript. It never surfaced during Mahmud's lifetime. Meanwhile, the *Shahnama* had been distributed throughout the realm and become a sensation.

Sometime later, Mahmud was besieging a stronghold. As he rode with an officer to parlay over a possible truce with the enemy, he wondered aloud what the other side could possibly offer. The officer recited the lines of the *Shahnama*:

> Should the answer come contrary to my wish
> then for me the mace and the arena of Afrasiab.

"Whose verse is that?" asked the sultan. "He must have the heart of a man."

"He who labored for five and twenty years to complete such a work and reaped for it no advantage," replied the officer.

"You speak well," said Mahmud. "I deeply regret that this noble man was disappointed in me. Remind me at Ghazni to send him something."

Back in Ghazni, Mahmud wrote an apology to Firdawsi and sent a shipment of indigo worth sixty thousand dinars (gold coins) to him. But as the delivering caravan entered one of the city gates, the bier carrying Firdawsi's corpse was being carried out through another. His daughter was taking his body to be buried in his garden outside the town. When she was approached, she proudly rejected the sultan's gift.

From that day to this, the great sultan who conquered nations and laid the foundation for the future Muslim empires in India is chiefly remembered not for his accomplishments, but for his insult to Persia's greatest poet—and the apology that came too late.

▶ **Remember: An apology delayed is an offense compounded. When you need to apologize, don't fret over it. Be deliberate, be sincere, and be fast.**

part five

MAKING EVEN YOUR HANDICAPS
WORK FOR YOU

The Secret Plan That Elected Kennedy

When stuck with a lemon, make lemonade

Facile minds go into high gear when they work to turn a liability into an asset. A good real-estate agent stuck with a house next to a busy railway line will advertise it as a "commuter's dream." A movie agent stuck with an actor with a cleft chin and pockmarks will stress his rugged look. A salesperson with an outmoded product will talk about its proven record of reliability.

These maneuvers are so obvious and so common we barely give them a second thought. But sometimes the maneuver is not so obvious. In the election of 1960 it was disguised so brilliantly that even now most historians and political journalists are unaware of it.

The 1960 election is widely recognized as a turning point in American politics. The election of a Catholic to the presidency broke one of the strongest taboos in a country that considered itself a Protestant nation. The election of 1928 had confirmed this taboo when the solidly Democratic South broke its party allegiance to elect Republican Herbert Hoover over Catholic Al Smith of New York.

Few born after 1960 can conceive of how deeply the prejudice ran: Protestant leaders such as Norman Vincent Peale were honestly concerned that a Catholic president would put himself at the beck and call of the pope. They freely used their pulpits to warn of the prospect. In even the most enlightened Southern cities, where Protestants intermingled freely with such alien species as Jews and Mormons in business and society, children were not allowed to play with Catholic neighbors for fear of their contaminating dogmas. On quarters, George Washington's head was painted over in nail polish with a red skullcap so that nobody would miss the point of the coming domination of Rome (never mind that the pope's skullcap is white).

By 1960 only four states in the Union could muster Catholic majorities: New York, Rhode Island, Connecticut, and John F. Kennedy's home state of Massachusetts. If religion were allowed to dominate the campaign, the Democratic candidate would surely go down to a blazing defeat.

The Democrats needed a way to keep the election from focusing on Kennedy's religion. With Reformation Sunday, a day which many Protestant ministers took as an occasion to remind their congregations of the evils of the Church of Rome, falling on October 30— just a week before the election—something needed to be done.

The opportunity came on September 12, 1960. John Kennedy made the decision to address the Greater Houston Ministerial Association and to confront the Catholic question head-on in front of a Protestant audience. His brilliant speech reaffirming the separation of church and state is said by some historians to rank with Lincoln's "A House Divided" and William Jennings Bryan's "Cross of Gold" speeches. Its enthusiastic reception by the ministers was widely played up in newspapers and on television, and it put the matter of religion to rest. Kennedy went on to win the election by the narrowest margin in history, and his achievement over religious prejudice became a catalyst for the civil rights movement that was to dominate the rest of the decade.

That, at least, is the official story as told by political scientists and historians. The 1960 election was indeed a turning point, but not in the way we've been led to believe.

The 1960 election was the first in which sophisticated computer analysis of key demographic voting groups was used by the winning side to secure victory. That computer analysis led to Kennedy's secret game plan of making a speech in defense of the political rights of his co-religionists. His purpose was not to mollify Protestant fears, as was reported at the time and has been accepted ever since. Instead his secret purpose was to galvanize the Catholic vote.

By 1960, Catholics had a higher representation in the House of Representatives than any other denomination; Catholic governors had been elected in the key states of California and Ohio; and Catholic voters made up more than twenty-five percent of the electorate, with commanding presences in fourteen of the largest states. Compared to 1928, the America of 1960 was a far different—and far more Catholic—country.

A professor by the name of Ithiel de Sola Pool at the Massachusetts Institute of Technology in Boston had been experimenting with computer simulation techniques as a predictive device for several years when his work was brought to the attention of Robert Kennedy in 1959. The younger Kennedy was quick to grasp how the professor's work could be applied to elective politics. At his urging, de Sola Pool divided the voting population into 480 "clusters" based on common characteristics—for example, urban black unmarried females. While the major media were touting generalized national polls that showed the race to be dead-even, Robert Kennedy instructed his pollsters to concentrate on the clusters to identify his brother's strengths and weaknesses; de Sola Pool's computer simulation then projected the polling results into a national vote total.

By August of 1960 de Sola Pool's simulation showed that Kennedy would lose by a tiny margin in the popular vote but by a much larger margin in the electoral college. The reason? He had failed to make a dint in one small segment of the vote that would push several important states into the Republican column: Southern male Republican Catholics.

Now the question in late August was, What to do? Nixon and the Republicans had judiciously refrained from using the religious question and had taken firm measures to squelch anyone who tried. The issue of Kennedy's Catholicism was off-limits.

For Kennedy to have a chance of winning, the question of whether a Catholic could be a good American had to somehow get back into the headlines. Campaign managers learned of the Houston ministers' meeting scheduled for September. It was the perfect forum. They made a last-minute decision to send Kennedy there.

If nobody else was going to raise the Catholic question, Kennedy would have to do it himself: by denouncing it.

The ploy worked. Democratic pollsters reported immediately that Catholic Republicans and Independents felt Kennedy's speech had been a defense of their own patriotism. He squeaked by in Texas by a margin of 50.8 percent (provided, as one wit put it, "by live Catholics and dead Protestants"—a reference to suspicious votes cast in notorious Duval County). In Nelson County, Kentucky, he won five previously Republican but heavily Catholic precincts by a margin of 85 percent. Similar results were reported in places as different as Philadelphia and Los Angeles.

The closest popular election in American history had been saved for the Democrats by a mathematics professor. He had seen John Kennedy's greatest liability for what it really was: the asset that could put him over the top. And the ploy has largely been a secret ever since.

▶ Remember: Your chief liability might actually be an asset. Try redefining it, then using it. You don't want to be stuck eating that lemon.

The Puny
Champion of France

Discount your disabilities, and get on with the job

Benjamin Disraeli was the first member of his race to be elected to the British House of Commons, and in the England of that time his election caused a commotion. Even though Disraeli had converted to Anglicanism as a teenager, he remained well aware that his Hebrew heritage was a distinct disadvantage. But he did not shirk from it. On one occasion in 1837, when Disraeli was a newly elected member of Parliament, the Irish leader Daniel O'Connell attacked him bitterly in the House, and in the course of his assault referred to Disraeli's Jewish background.

The young Disraeli rose to reply, "Yes, I am a Jew, and when the ancestors of the right honorable gentleman were brutal savages on an unknown island, mine were priests in the temple of Solomon." Three decades later that same proud Jew was elected prime minister of Great Britain.

Disabilities come in every kind: background, class, race, physical handicaps, psychological makeup, financial means—and the list goes on. The longer the list, the more it seems that not many of us were born without one.

Bertrand du Guesclin was born so ugly and puny a baby that his parents, the lord and lady of a minor castle in Brittany, preferred not to see him—ever.

He was so neglected during his childhood that he could never be sure of the exact date of his birth (thought to be around 1320). Unlike other nobles of similar station, his education was so paltry that later in life he was said to have had trouble signing his name. Even though he was the eldest son and therefore lawful heir to the estate, his mother gave him no training in the social graces nor did his father in the art of war, the only two things for which the nobility existed. Instead, ugly little Bertrand spent most of his early life among the only people who would pay any attention to him, the kitchen staff. His education in how to fight came from neighborhood boys with whom he played—and from whom he learned skills that were never taught to any noble.

At the age of seventeen he appeared out of nowhere in Rennes at a brilliantly attended tournament, riding a shaggy plow horse and so ill-armed that the herald supervising the event denied him entry. Bertrand appealed to a nearby kinsman who took pity and equipped him in a more knightly fashion. Clad in borrowed armor he entered the lists and proceeded to sweep them, disarming his opponents with moves they had never seen before. At the day's conclusion, when he rode up to the judge's stand and lifted his visor, his parents were astonished to discover that the diminutive teenage champion was their son.

Years went by and Bertrand was still winning almost every contest or war he entered. He didn't win every time (the king of France ransomed him on several occasions, which may be why that king is remembered as Charles the Wise), but so much more than any one else ever had that his fame spread throughout Europe. His prowess became so legendary, and his tactical skills so invaluable, that the king appointed him Constable of France, in command of all the king's forces, and, for good measure, Count of Longueville, and the king of Castile made him Duke of Molina. He was rich beyond his parents' imaginings.

But that was not all. Bertrand was adored by women. He never courted any, perhaps too aware of how he looked. But they courted him—his superiority on the field seemed to stir something more than admiration. And finally it won him a wife.

While commanding the defense of Dinan against the English, Bertrand was outraged when the English violated a truce by capturing his brother. When the English demanded a large ransom for his brother's return, Bertrand was further incensed. The insult of an unchivalrous deed was now doubled, and the great knight would have none of it. Bertrand instead challenged his brother's captor to single combat. The English knight was, of course, tall and handsome. Short, ugly Bertrand defeated the Englishman handily. The training of knighthood taught all the lessons of armor, weaponry, horses, and method, and the Englishman no doubt knew all those. But Bertrand, from his roughhousing with the neighborhood warriors of his childhood, had learned a greater lesson—tactics.

For his feat at Dinan, Bertrand received a double bonus: the French king gave him the ransom due to the English, and the English gave Bertrand back his brother.

The third bonus was completely unexpected. As it turned out, practically all the people of Dinan were on the walls to watch the match between the champions, including the learned, highly cultivated, and beautiful Tiphaine Raguenel, a young noblewoman of the city. She was so impressed by the exploit that she began negotiating to marry the ugly little knight. Their improbable union, which fascinated France, took four years to arrange. One suspects parental objections as the reason for the delay, but then again maybe Bertrand himself was suspicious at the reason for this sudden infatuation. But Tiphaine had her way, and the two were wed when Bertrand was about forty-one.

The lovely and beloved Tiphaine died three years later, leaving the warrior bereft. Bertrand was by then an almost legendary figure to his contemporaries. He had defeated the English in the second phase of what would become known as the Hundred Years War, and a grateful king had heaped upon him honors and estates.

But that is not what gained him a new wife. Nineteen years before, Bertrand had defeated all comers in a particularly bloody tournament at the magnificent castle of Montmuran. The owners of the castle, the Lavals, were one of the oldest and richest families in France. Watching in the stands, a young daughter had been dazzled by Bertrand's performance and after the contest was thrilled to watch him formally dubbed a knight. Now that Bertrand was a widower, Jeanne-Anne de Laval proposed to marry him.

Their marriage lasted until Bertrand's death. Despite her wealth and prestige, Jeanne-Anne never remarried, and she lived to an old age rare in medieval times. We know of her longevity because it is recorded that in 1429, forty-nine years after Bertrand's death, Joan of Arc sent Jeanne-Anne a ring as a token of respect for her departed husband, Joan's hero and France's champion.

When Joan had her headquarters at Saint-Denis in the summer of 1429 she must have paused at his tomb in the abbey church, where his effigy is finely carved. She may have reflected, as any modern visitor can, on how small this giant was.

▶ Remember: Your only handicap is your opinion of yourself. If you think you are weak, or stupid, or maimed, or downtrodden, you are. Puny, ugly Bertrand never seemed to have thought about his disabilities. He set out to be the best—and so can you.

The Wife of Jesus

Always fail upward, toward higher and higher goals

An aide congratulated the Greek king Pyrrhus on his victory over the Romans. Pyrrhus mournfully replied, "One more victory such as that, and we are undone." He had lost as many men in winning as the enemy had in losing, and now had none to spare. But the Romans were an unending wave, and they would come again.

The Pyrrhic victory, which is really a loss, has its counterbalance in the failure that leads to success. Howard Hughes' famous attempt at a new airplane, the ill-named *Spruce Goose,* was also ill-fated (it never flew higher than five hundred feet), but it led to revolutionary developments in aeronautics that produced our modern concept of aircraft design. Edison thought he had failed to invent a telephone-answering machine when he discarded the phonograph as unworkable; only later did he discover that he'd invented the music-recording industry. The fiery abolitionist John Brown failed at freeing the slaves, but his raid at Harpers Ferry inflamed the South and helped ignite the Civil War. Notable failures have time and again brought consequences as far-reaching as most successes.

Catherine of Siena was probably as great a failure as history has ever known.

Vivacious and attractive, she was the twenty-third child (which even then must have been a record, and she had a little sister!) of a modestly respectable wool-processing family. Her life as a child was amid the lively company of her vocal neighbors and her brothers and sisters, who made up most of her father's workforce. Looming over her closely packed, lower-middle-class Sienese neighborhood was the Gothic church of San Domenico, served by Dominican friars whose gentleness and selflessness apparently made quite an impression on her. At the age of seven she announced to her mother that instead of marrying one of the normal neighbor boys someday, she intended to become the wife of Jesus. Her mother slapped her for such impudence, but her father thought she was charming. At the age of seventeen, Catherine got her way. She became a nun.

The twenty-third child of a boisterous family is not likely to be a conventional nun. Sure enough, Catherine was soon re-creating family life in the cloister, attracting men and women of all classes, most of them older than she, who came to her for spiritual advice. Her *Caterinati* began to act as though they constituted a new (and entirely unauthorized) religious order. To keep in touch with the active and mobile members of this highly unusual *famiglia,* which included merchants, artists, and soldiers, Catherine began to dictate a series of letters that soon brought her to the attention of higher authorities in the Dominican order and even the papacy. The Dominicans assigned a learned friar to become her confessor (and in that capacity, to control her). He quickly succumbed to her charm, declared himself her spiritual son, and became her spokesman and champion.

Catherine seems to have been utterly unfazed by the deck that had been stacked against her. Her background was entirely provincial in a time when provincialism meant not caring about doings in the next neighborhood, much less the next city. She grew up in a society so man-centered that religious life was the only escape for any lowborn woman of talent. And by the standards of the day, her modest family was lowborn, with no privilege or inheritance and no prospect of either. She was probably not even fully literate.

But there is no doubt that she knew her own mind, and she wasn't afraid to give others a piece of it—even if it meant upbraiding the Holy Father himself.

Catherine was scandalized that the popes of her time lived in Avignon in France instead of Rome, the proper diocese of the man who was, after all, bishop of Rome. She was also affronted by papal diplomacy that encouraged the recurring warfare among the city-states of her native Italy (John XXII just two decades before she was born had devoted sixty percent of papal revenues to his military budget). In the 1370s she began writing Pope Gregory XI letters of astonishing bluntness, telling him in effect to shape up. When no reply came, Catherine left her cloister at Siena to travel to Avignon to confront him face-to-face, preaching her message at every stop through northern Italy and southern France.

Moved by Catherine's intensity and her personal magnetism, Gregory XI returned the papacy to Rome in 1377. The twenty-nine-year-old Catherine went along, strengthening the pontiff's resolution in the face of his enemies, sometimes literally holding him by the hand in moments of decision, pulling him along as if he were an aged father. When the election following his death in 1378 produced the Great Schism (for the next thirty-one years there were two rival popes, one at Avignon and one at Rome, and for eight years after that there were three), Catherine retired in grief from public life.

She had been an utter failure—except that her crusade had saved the papacy. In preaching so loudly and insistently about the wrongs done to the throne of St. Peter, she instilled among the disillusioned a renewed reverence for the holiness of the office, if not for the men who claimed to hold it. That deep veneration outlasted the schisms and caused their end, for finally the whole world rose to demand that the secular powers stop their meddling and the papacy be restored as the unifying office of all Catholic Christendom.

In the last two years of her life, Catherine returned to the role of mother of her far flung *famiglia* and dictated her spiritual testament. That powerful statement of candid and lyrical piety, along with her collected letters, describes her "mystical marriage" with Jesus in terms so moving that generations of artists and formally trained theologians have been equally inspired by it. Just one hundred years after her death she was named a saint, and in time she became the patron saint of Italy. In 1970 Paul VI went so far as to name this barely literate nun as one of the Doctors of the Church, a distinction held only by a dozen of its greatest thinkers, putting Catherine in the company of such titans as St. Augustine and St. Thomas Aquinas.

But Catherine in life would not have been impressed with the honors she received after her death. In 1380, while she was in Rome, she experienced an ecstatic vision so great she could not resist it, and she died. It is said that she had finally seen her husband, and contemporaries had no doubt that she was happy to die at the age she did. She was thirty-three, the same age as Jesus at the time of the crucifixion.

▶ **Remember: In her failure Catherine made the whole world focus on her goal. She was direct, consistent, and bold—and always charming. What failure has stopped you? Was it a great enough failure that the world will be changed by it? Then was it really a failure at all, or just one of life's setbacks? A setback causes us to change ourselves, but a great failure can change the world.**

The Accidental Architect

If you are different, use your difference to see what others can't

Most architects are well aware of the dangers of originality. Francesco Borromini was an innovator in the new Baroque style of his time, but for the great vaulted arches of St. Peter's he drew on the ruins of the monumental market basilica in the Roman

Forum. Michelangelo was one of the world's most original minds, but to design St. Peter's huge dome he studied the ancient—and larger—dome of the Pantheon. Architectural ideas skip from generation to generation, and architectural styles are recycled over the centuries. But when and where they originate is almost impossible to pinpoint. What was the first Classical Greek temple, for example, or the first Baroque palace? Who built the first Federal house, or designed the first Greek Revival bank building?

The modernist school of Le Corbusier, Mies van der Rohe, Frank Lloyd Wright, and others was an original response to the possibilities that arose from the availability of new materials, but even it contained deliberate echoes of earlier styles. (And the response didn't always work. A client once angrily telephoned Frank Lloyd Wright: "Frank!" he bellowed. "We're sitting at the dinner table, and your roof is leaking right onto the top of my head." "Hmm," replied Wright thoughtfully, "why don't you move your chair?")

The new material of the twelfth century was stained glass. Romanesque churches had begun installing stained-glass windows more than a century before. The earliest extant examples are larger-than-life Old Testament figures in the windows of Augsburg Cathedral, dating from about 1050. But the old architecture couldn't really handle this new art—the colored glass only emphasized the darkness of the interior. What was needed was a new form, something that would give full play to the light and colors these new windows created.

The new architectural style called for by the invention of stained glass was created by one man. The building was the royal abbey church of Saint-Denis, and its builder was one Abbot Suger—a man with no known architectural background. The style is now known as Gothic architecture, but the term was imposed by snobbish art critics in the Italian Renaissance as a slur on nonclassical styles. Medieval people called the style "modern," and considering its radical departure from anything that had come before, we should understand why.

From what we know about Abbot Suger, he seems to have been an administrative genius who rose not only to head his own abbey but also to become the king's first minister. Michel Bur, Suger's most recent biographer and an authority on medieval social history, is convinced that Suger was born a peasant.

But of one thing there is no doubt: the abbot was very short, even for his time. A generation earlier, William the Conquerer at five-foot-ten towered over his contemporaries. Three hundred years later, Joan of Arc would seem a perfectly normal-sized young woman at five-foot-two. The good abbot was well under five feet tall.

Given to the abbey by his devout family when he was seven, Suger soon showed signs of exception intelligence, and despite his lowly background, he was put on the fast track to clerical preferment. Perhaps his short stature led him to work harder than his taller classmates. Whatever the reason, he was made prior of an outlying monastery at the age of twenty-seven, and before he reached forty was elected abbot of the great house of Saint-Denis.

The abbot's administrative talents were put to good use by Louis VI, who relied on him to reorganize the state. On the king's death, his son Louis VII was somewhat put off by Suger's influence in his newly inherited realm, but even so recognized his abilities well enough to make him regent of France in 1147 when he went off to fight the Second Crusade.

Meanwhile, Suger decided to do something dramatic to enhance his new monarch's international prestige. His idea was to expand the royal abbey church in a radical new way. He enlisted two (some art scholars say three) of the most daring "modern" architects practicing in the 1140s. (The time had not yet come when architects or artists signed their work, so we can't even guess at their names.) Whoever these draftsmen were, the vision was the abbot's. One story recounts how the builders told him that beams of the length he wanted for a certain roof could never be found because trees just didn't grow that tall. The diminutive monk ordered them to follow him out into the forest, and after a day's searching, twelve trees were found. The abbot knew what he wanted.

William Clark, the foremost authority on Saint-Denis and Gothic architecture, insists that the brilliance of this vision lay not with such new techniques as flying buttresses; these were merely means of making it work. The real genius lay in an entirely new conception of how to illuminate and expand the space within a building. The result was something dazzlingly new. No known patron in the history of art has ever been as drastically innovative.

What allowed or caused Abbot Suger to break with convention with such confidence and even exuberance? We know he was a major art collector. Clearly he was also a genuine executive who knew how to coordinate money, manpower, and materials on a schedule. He had a great ego, as we can tell from the dozens of inscriptions he carved or nailed into his new church. But the secret to his passionate willingness to invest everything in this radical new form may be found in one of the stained-glass windows in the ambulatory at the eastern end of his church. It is a visually magnificent and learned window, full of references to Church history and biblical scholarship. And at the bottom of it, prostrate with hands upraised to higher truth, lies the figure of a very small monk. No mystery about who he is. The glass itself tells us: *Sugerius*, the inscription reads.

Here is one very short person who found a way to tower above all his contemporaries.

▶ Remember: Suger may have been short, but his vision was large. Did his shortness make him want to create something tall? Could you use the qualities that make you different to see what others miss?

The Barbarian Who Created France

Use the codes of the old culture to change it

Those who are successful in changing a culture first take care to understand the culture they want to change. Every company, every organization, every family, has its own distinctive culture. Remaking that culture can't be done by attempting to remake the codes that are embedded in it. Those very codes are the weapons that make change possible, if they are cleverly employed as instruments of change.

No consultant could have predicted what Jack Welch accomplished when he took over the helm at General Electric at the age of forty-five in 1981. GE was already an industrial giant, of course, but like most giants it was slow and clumsy. Foreign competition and new technologies inflicted a thousand cuts while GE lumbered on, scarcely recognizing that it was hurt and bleeding to death. Welch whipped the company back into fighting shape. He eliminated layers of bureaucracy, cast off old technologies, invested in new ones, and insisted that in whatever GE undertook it would be the best. Welch was able to shape up GE because he was steeped in GE values and in the mind-set of the managers he needed to change. They wanted autonomy; he gave it back to them. They hated red tape; he did away with it. They were once accustomed to dominating their markets; he demanded that they dominate or he'd discard the whole division. GE today ranks number one among American companies, with a market capitalization of some $200 billion.

In a quite different case, outsider Lou Gerstner came into an IBM that was reeling after being rudely shoved off its perch atop the technological heap. Gerstner took the time to understand that pride was an essential part of the IBM ethos, and that the company's pride had declined as severely as its bottom line. He carefully invested in such projects as Big Blue, the computer that beat the chess masters, to beef up his company's morale. By restoring its pride, he has restored IBM's fortunes.

Fifteen hundred years earlier a barbarian warlord wanted to change the tribal culture that kept his kinsmen from achieving distinction among the civilized peoples of Europe. By succeeding he created a race that would become the nation of France.

Most of the barbarian leaders who swept through the remains of the Roman Empire in the fourth and fifth centuries saw little more in its wealth and grandeur than a prime opportunity for plunder and pillage. Clovis, war chief of the Franks, saw something more. Clovis had ambition. He wanted to be a king, to combine his rough tribesmen with the civilized Gallo-Romans, and so to rule the rich lands of Gaul.

The people whom Clovis wanted to lead were Christians, and he would not be accepted as their legitimate king unless he too became a Christian. That, of course, was easy enough to do—unless one happened to be war chief of the pagan Franks. To become a Christian himself, he would have to bring his whole tribe to Christianity. That would not only be difficult but dangerous.

Clovis seems to have developed his strategy at an early age. In his youth he corresponded with Remigius, archbishop of Reims and spiritual head of the Gallic Church, and seems to have hinted at his ultimate goal broadly enough to enlist the great archbishop as a hopeful ally. His choice of a wife seems equally calculated. The princess Clothilde of Burgundy was not only royal but also a staunch Catholic, a signal that must have pleased Clovis' clerical correspondent in Reims. But there remained the problem of his intractably pagan Franks.

Reassuring the Christian establishment while keeping control over his restless tribe required cunning and nerve. He would have to make the warrior values of his tribe work for him, and paramount among those values were loyalty to the chief, respect for the tribe's traditions, and the inviolability of oaths given and received.

In 486, shortly after becoming war chief, Clovis led an assault against Soissons, the stronghold of the Gallo-Roman army that had been protecting the Seine valley against barbarian invasion for a generation. The Franks had sometimes served as mercenaries for that army against other Germanic tribes, but in pursuit of his larger plan to rule all of Gaul, Clovis decided his erstwhile allies must be subdued.

When the victory was won, all the booty from the captured city was heaped in one great pile outside its walls, in accordance with Frankish custom, ready for distribution to the war band. The bishop of Soissons approached the young war chief and asked him to save from desecration the sacred vessels used in celebrating Mass. In line with his policy of placating the Christians, Clovis agreed.

As war leader, Clovis had the right to the largest share of the booty, but his turn came last. He asked his men if anyone would mind his taking the bishop's gold chalice to begin with. One crude old warrior immediately objected, accusing him of consorting with the Christians, and when his turn came picked the chalice for himself, throwing it on the ground and smashing it with one blow from his *francisca*, the distinctive iron tomahawk of the Franks. Clovis did nothing. The bishop understood that the young chieftain had to respect Frankish custom and appreciated the effort.

Some time later, as his troops tumbled out of their tents to line up for a dawn review, Clovis encountered the foul-tempered warrior who had shamed him at Soissons. He berated the rough warrior, grabbed his helmet, and threw it to the ground. When the warrior bent to pick the helmet up, the *francisca* in Clovis' right hand swept up and then down to cleave the warrior's skull. "Remember the cup of Soissons," Clovis said to his men, and they did (and French schoolchildren do to this day). His authority was now total.

Having made one point, Clovis now looked for an opportunity to score a bigger one. It came when he went against another Germanic tribe, the Alamanni, who had invaded territory the Franks claimed as their own. At the height of the battle, Clovis rose in his stirrups and shouted at the top of this voice, "God of Clothilde, give me this battle, and I give you my people." Almost all scholars of the period are convinced Clovis already knew the day was his. With this great shout, he seized the moment to convert his people.

Now becoming Christian was a matter of keeping his oath, as any Frank would agree. The warrior code demanded it.

Clovis wanted his acceptance into the Church to be as ostentatious as possible. He marched into the cathedral at Reims at the head of a host of captains and tribal leaders. Forewarned, Archbishop Remigius had decked out the church with candles and fine curtains. With great solemnity and ritual, to give these barbarian ruffians some hint of the power and beauty of the Holy Spirit, the archbishop led Clovis to the wading pool. He then instructed the Frankish war chief to bow his proud neck meekly to receive the blessing of baptism. When the pouring of the water was done, Remigius declared to the young chieftain that he must now "worship what he had burned, and burn what he had worshiped." Oath-bound to their chief, the Frankish captains had no choice but to follow his lead. They shouted their approval, and one by one marched forward to submit to the new religion. By nightfall, the Franks had become the only Catholic Germanic tribe, and thus the prime barbarian allies of the pope and defenders of Gaul.

Clovis had achieved his goal. His Franks were now France in the making. Three hundred years later, his successor, in direct line, would aspire to an even greater goal of restoring the Roman Empire. His name was Charlemagne.

▶ Remember: Clovis changed his tribal culture not by squashing its customs (impossible) or even trying to reform them (hazardous) but by using them to gain his own goal, so that change when it came was not resisted but endorsed.

The Lieutenant Nun

Know your limitations, but don't be bound by them

Man is the creature that makes excuses. Louis XV once confronted Mme d'Esparbes, one of his mistresses, with the fact that she had slept with the Duc de Choiseul. "Yes, sire, but he is so powerful!" What about the Marechel de Richelieu, the king persisted. "But he is so witty!" And Mainville? "He has such beautiful legs!" Then what about Duc d'Aumont, who possesses none of those attractions? "But he is so loyal to Your Majesty!"

Excuses can be used as convenient tools to explain away our incapacities. One wonders how many sentences have begun with "If only I had more money . . ." or "If only I were younger . . ." The sympathetic listeners might nod and agree and say, "Yes, if only . . ." but no one is fooling anybody. The achievers of this world ignore and even defy the limitations imposed on them.

Catalina de Erauso lived in an age when a woman's choices were either to get married or enter a nunnery. But she wasn't religious or particularly interested in a placid, domestic life. On the contrary, she was adventurous, hot-tempered, and determined. She wanted to explore the world and become one of Spain's most famous soldiers. She wasn't about to say, "If only I were a man . . ."

Catalina was born in 1585 in San Sebastian and placed in the local Dominican convent for schooling at the age of six. If a husband was not found for her by the time she was of marrying age, she would join the order. Catalina was not one to pay much attention to other people's expectations. At the age of fifteen she somehow got hold of some men's clothes, donned them as a disguise, and slipped out of the nunnery. Her family never heard from her again. She made her way to Seville—now relishing her newly clothed virility—and talked her way aboard a ship bound for the New World.

In Panama and then in Peru, she worked as a merchant's apprentice, and by then her masculine impersonation was well practiced and complete. Later in Lima, the government began to recruit soldiers to fight against the Araucanian Indians in Chile. Catalina enlisted and was sent to Concepción on the Chilean coast. There she discovered the governor's secretary was Miguel de Erauso, an older brother she had never known. She did not reveal her identity, but told him she was from his hometown and knew his family. Miguel was so pleased to meet a neighbor he invited her to stay with him. He introduced her to his mistress, and the two became close friends. After a while Miguel began to get jealous of the friendship between his lover and this handsome young man from his hometown, so he had the soldier shipped out to the front.

Catalina—decked out now in a uniform—found herself in a long campaign against the Indians. In the last bloody skirmish the Indians made a daring attack on the headquarters, killed many of the staff officers, and carried off the regimental standard. As they retreated, Catalina went after them, slashing her way through their ranks until she got to—and killed—their chieftain. She grabbed the standard and, wounded but still mobile, fought her way back to the Spanish lines. By the time she reached safety she carried three arrows in various parts of her body. The exploit got her promoted to lieutenant, though she was barely twenty years old (and, of course, a woman, which nobody knew).

When Catalina was reassigned to Concepción her flaring temper caught up with her. In a gambling den, she stabbed a fellow officer who she suspected was cheating at cards. She was hauled before the magistrate, but when he tried to restrain her, she slashed his face and fought her way to safety. Later that night she was asked to be the second of a fellow officer in a duel. The two parties met, but the duel had barely begun when Catalina's friend was struck and killed. Enraged, she attacked his opponent and his second, and blindly killed both of them, only to discover that she had murdered her brother. She was the only survivor that night.

Devastated, she hid in a nearby Franciscan church. The governor was furious and put a price on her head. A friend slipped her money and a horse, and Catalina fled over the Andes. Newly arrived in Argentina, she enlisted in the local militia and became a fast friend of the sergeant major. They battled and brawled their way up and down the countryside for two years before the authorities decided their lawlessness was worse than the outlaws they were supposed to be after. Catalina was days away from a trip to the scaffold when she escaped again, making her way to Guamanga, Peru.

The year was 1620. True to form, she managed to involve herself in a scuffle in Guamanga soon after she arrived, this time in the cathedral square. The bishop heard the commotion, looked out his window to see a young man resisting arrest, and, with some difficulty, managed to draw the man inside the church. He locked the door behind him and ordered supper to be brought to his quarters. He would get to the heart of this matter himself, he decided.

The bishop wanted to know how the young man had gotten to Guamanga. At first, the man blustered through a well-rehearsed story of himself as a soldier of fortune. But under the prelate's gentle prodding, the young man finally confessed that he was not a man at all. In fact, he was a woman named Catalina. And she had hustled, gambled, soldiered, and murdered her way throughout the Spanish Empire's Wild West.

The bishop thought the story was ludicrous. Catalina volunteered to prove her sex if the bishop would summon his housekeepers to examine her. The women were as astonished as the bishop to confirm that this creature was indeed a woman—and a virgin, to boot. The bishop ordered her confined to the convent of Santa Clara while he pondered the matter and received counsel from the government in Lima. After some time she was summoned to the capital. There, *"la monja alferez"* ("the lieutenant nun") stirred a sensation. She was sheltered in a convent again for nearly three years while details of her story were confirmed in Spain. When her tale was proven true, she was set free.

Her travels were not over. Back in Spain she planned to go to Rome, probably as a penance. She took the land route and was attacked and robbed in Piedmont. Begging her way back to Barcelona, she threw herself on the mercy of the king. He had heard of her remarkable life and teased her for being out-fought by a gang of bandits. But when she told him her assailants were nine men with guns, he quadrupled her pension and sent her on her way.

In Rome, she was warmly received by Pope Urban VIII, who was so intrigued by her stories that he invited her to stay for six weeks, dining every night in the palaces of princes and prelates. Cardinal Magalon was one of the many who were intrigued by her adventures, remarking that her only fault was her Spanish blood, which caused the always-explosive Catalina to reply, "With all due respect, Your Eminence, that is my only *virtue!*"

▶ Remember: Your limitations may be real, but they also may be imagined. If Catalina is any example, anything you can dream, you can do.

The Courtier Who Became a God

Use a loss in one arena to help you succeed in another

Any student of baseball will become a philosopher at an early age. Only two or three seasons teach the hard lesson that in life things do not always work out. The national pastime, in this respect, has always been out of sync with the national psyche. Sociologists have come to call this the theory of relief. In other words, success-driven, anxious Americans need a break.

America is a society in total thrall to its winners, whether they're moguls, mobsters, or this month's movie stars. Japan, on the other hand, is a society fascinated by its losers. No wonder it is the only other major country where baseball has really caught on.

Sugawara Michizane was neither a military genius nor a great statesman, yet after his death he was elevated to a deity (in the Shinto religion, something between a demigod and a Christian patron saint), and his cult has lasted to this day. Most modern Japanese know him as Tenjin, the patron deity of calligraphy, classical learning, and political reform. Today parents pray that Tenjin will help their children do well with their studies.

He was a master of calligraphy, and by hereditary right a tutor of classical Chinese literature at the imperial court. But these were the standard earmarks of a gentleman in his day. His principal occupation was as a courtier in the imperial court, where he worked tirelessly to restore the ancient prerogatives of the emperor against the scheming nobility. These efforts at political reform, which brought him down and sent him into exile, he made elegiac with poetry, which in turn endeared him to the Japanese heart.

The imperial family had been long eclipsed in power by the rise of feudal clans, and in 858 the most powerful of these, the Fujiwara, assumed power by taking over simultaneously the offices of regent and chancellor, as well as command of the army. The emperor was now only a figurehead, a condition that was to last for the next one thousand years.

Emperor Uda resisted the Fujiwara usurpation. His goal was not only to reign but to rule, and Michizane was his principal minister in the intrigues and maneuvers against the rival Fujiwara court. The opposition to the emperor's ambition was fierce. His only weapon was his prestige as the direct descendant of the sun goddess Amaterasu. While this was considerable enough to allow him to keep his head, it wasn't enough to allow him to keep his throne. In 901 the emperor accepted early retirement in favor of his presumably more pliant son. His right-hand man, Michizane, was banished to Kyushu, the southernmost of the four main islands of the Japanese archipelago.

There the exiled courtier spent the better part of his days facing east toward the capital in front of a box with the chrysanthemum crest of the emperor on its top, containing the robes of the minister of the right, a reminder of his once-exalted position. In such a posture he would recite one of the melancholy poems he was composing, which have since made him one of the supreme figures in Japanese literature:

Now that I have become
Mere scum that floats upon the water's face,
May you, my lord, become a weir
And stop me in my downward flow.

After his death in 903 his poems became so popular that even Fujiwara power could not prevent the reigning emperor from ordering the construction of a shrine to honor the beloved family retainer at Kitano ("the Heavenly Fields"), just north of Kyoto. Having lost position and power, Michizane had nowhere to turn but to poetry, and his poems elevated him into the pantheon of the deities.

Only one other Shinto deity—the god of war—has more shrines than Tenjin in contemporary Japan. Happily, Tenjin draws more pilgrims.

▶ Remember: Losing is as inevitable in life as it is in baseball. But loss in one realm may only prefigure accomplishment in another. Rely like Michizane on your gifts. What looks like a setback today may be your ticket to immortality.

part six

FINDING THE RIGHT ANSWERS

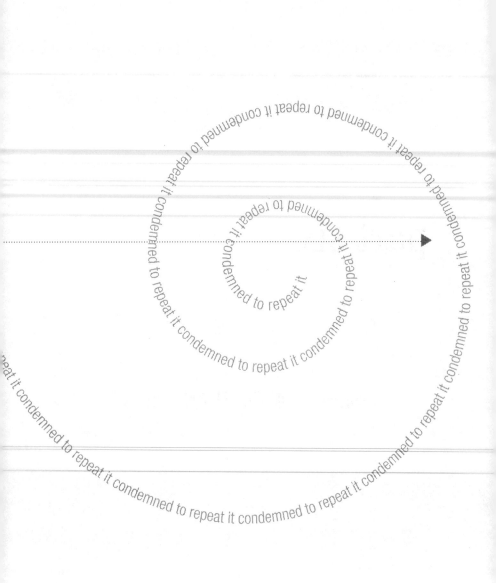

condemned to repeat it condemned to repeat it condemned to repeat it condemned to repeat it condemned to repeat it condemned to repeat it condemned to repeat it condemned to repeat it condemned to repeat it condemned to repeat it condemned to repeat it condemned to repeat it condemned to repeat it condemned to repeat it condemned to repeat it condemned to repeat it

The Photographs That Proved Einstein's Theory

Test an idea before committing to it

Sometime around 250 B.C. the king of Syracuse decided he wanted a crown made of gold, so he contracted with an artisan and supplied him with the precious metal from the treasury. Months later, when the artisan came back with the crown, the king was suspicious that the craftsman had substituted some silver for the gold, keeping the difference for himself. The king summoned the great philosopher and mathematician Archimedes to the palace, and asked if he could figure out whether the king had been cheated.

Archimedes pondered over the problem, but he couldn't figure out how to solve it. One evening as he was thinking the matter over, he slipped into a warm bath, filled to the brim. When the bathwater overflowed onto the floor, he leapt up. *"Eureka,"* he cried. *"Eureka*—I have found it!"

Archimedes had discovered the principle of fluid displacement, the fact that the weight of an irregular solid can be found by how much water it displaces. Gold being heavier than silver, the solution to his problem was at hand. After trying two or three other substances to establish a standard, he placed the crown in a large bowl of water, then reported to the king that he had indeed been cheated.

The scientific method was born, and its four pillars established: observation, theory, testing, proof.

In March 1919 two Royal Navy ships set sail from England, one for the west coast of Africa and another for the east coast of Brazil. Their purpose was to observe and photograph from the two sides of the Atlantic a solar eclipse that was to take place on May 29.

Aboard the Brazil-bound ship was a thirty-seven-year-old professor of astronomy at Cambridge. Arthur Eddington was well connected in the English scientific establishment, and he had worked those connections hard in lobbying for this expedition. The British government was in no mood—and in no position— to finance speculative ventures. The year before, Britain had suffered two hundred thousand casualties in the second battle of the Somme. As the tedious negotiations over the Treaty of Versailles ending World War I staggered on, the nation was exhausted and depleted. But Eddington was a persuasive man.

Eddington was also a man with a mission. The year before, he had published a paper, smuggled through the battle lines via the Netherlands, written by a German Jew named Albert Einstein. This paper, entitled "Gravitation and the Principle of Relativity," was perhaps the most eagerly awaited scientific paper ever published. Twelve years earlier, Einstein, then a clerk in a patent office in Switzerland, had written his first paper observing how lengths sometimes appear to shorten and time to slow down. Two years later, he had demonstrated that all mass contains energy, ending with the formula $E=mc^2$. The scientific world was abuzz at the revelations that seemed to flow with ease from this one man's mind. This latest paper had pulled together the different strands of his thought into an all-encompassing theory of physical law that was dazzling.

But Einstein saw himself as only a theorist. He made it plain that his work would have to be confirmed by experiments. He devised three tests that would either verify his theory or cause him to go back to the drawing board. The most important one required an eclipse to determine if a ray of light just grazing the surface of the sun would be bent by an arc of 1.75 seconds—more than twice what had been assumed before. If this calculation could be substantiated by firm evidence, then Einstein felt his theory of relativity would be worth pursuing.

On the morning of May 29 off the Príncipe Island, Eddington awoke to discover that a thunderstorm had moved in, obscuring everything. He and his colleagues paced the deck, incessantly asking the sailors questions about the wind and movement of the storm. The eclipse, the only one that would appear for the next three years, was to begin at 1:30 P.M. and end eight minutes later. At 1:29 the clouds moved on, leaving a clear view of the sun. Eddington had just eight minutes to work. As he recorded in his notebook at the time, "I did not see the eclipse, being too busy changing plates." He took sixteen photographs. For the next eight nights he developed the pictures at the rate of two a night. On June 3 he spent the entire day carefully measuring the first of the developed prints. That evening he emerged on deck to announce to his colleagues—and to the world—that Einstein was right.

The results of the expedition made headlines around the world. Overnight, Einstein became a popular hero. His insistence that his theory be subject to stringent tests and his willingness to accept that it might be untenable contrasted sharply with the dogmatism of quasi-scientists such as Marx or Freud. It showed the true scientific mind at work and raised science to a level of prestige that even the invention of the atom bomb could not dislodge.

Unhappily for Einstein, and much against his protests, the popular mind took the dissolution of the absolutes of time and space to mean all absolutes: good and evil, right and wrong, knowledge and ignorance, truth and untruth. As historian Paul Johnson puts it, "Mistakenly, but perhaps inevitably, relativity became confused with relativism." For that reason, he dates May 29, 1919, as the beginning of the modern world.

▶ **Remember: Anybody can have an idea. Whether it's worth anything is another question. You have to test your ideas. And to** do that you have to have the courage—and the humility—of an Einstein. Your ideas, after all, may be wrong.

The Philosopher Who Flunked Life

Think through the consequences

Poets and philosophers are rarely regarded as deadly. "A poet is a tamed beast, only left with words to claw at, in a cage of his own making," according to a two-thousand-year-old piece of Pompeian graffiti. Maybe that was true in Pompeii, but for the rest of history poets and philosophers have shown their power by the simple fact that words are remembered, and actions often aren't.

Two of the most famous poets in the English-speaking world, Percy Shelley and Lord Byron, have benefited from this dependence on the written word. Countless schoolchildren learn their verses, without ever being exposed to their lives. The lives might teach more than the poetry. These were two of the most ideological, reckless, foolish, vain, and deceitful men to ever capture the public's attention. Appropriately, they were among the world's first celebrities. And, appropriately again, they received their ideas from a disgruntled would-be philosopher, who at the time was as much a celebrity as they were. In fact, he was more famous than either of them.

The first great theoretical revolutionary wasn't Karl Marx. In 1793, more than fifty years before *The Communist Manifesto*, a thirty-seven-year-old schoolteacher named William Godwin created a sensation in England with a book entitled *Enquiry Concerning Political Justice*.

With an airy innocence that would be echoed by sixties radicals nearly two hundred years later, he argued that mankind is infinitely perfectible, and if only the twin evils of tradition and government could be overthrown, mankind would return to its natural virtue. In such a world "there would be no war, no crimes, no administration of justice . . ."

Unlike the Students for a Democratic Society in 1968, which managed to keep its founding statement to two pages, Godwin wrote on in this vein for two full volumes, abolishing as he went along disease, sleep, sex (in the interest of abolishing emotion), idleness, melancholy, lies, family, religion, and, finally, death. He seems to have relented a little on death by the second edition of 1796 (he was still against it, but his system might not totally eradicate it) and even on sex by the third edition of 1798 (maybe because by then he had been married twice). But he never thought these minor tinkerings affected the brilliance of his overall scheme.

Godwin became immediately famous as the leading English exponent of the French Revolution, which he believed would put his theories into practice and usher in a new age of harmony.

Fame brought him into contact with the equally famous Mary Wollstonecraft, and he was instantly smitten. She was a vivacious freethinker whose *Vindication of the Rights of Man* (in answer to Edmund Burke's masterly attack on the French Revolution) had established her radical credentials and whose *Vindication of the Rights of Woman* had established her feminist ones. If ever two people were meant for each other, this was it.

Despite his age Godwin had never before enjoyed a romantic relationship. Wollstonecraft was more a woman of the world; she brought with her to the affair an illegitimate child. The author who had condemned marriage as "the most odious of all monopolies" and the feminist who derided her sex's dependence on men carried on their relationship, fittingly enough, while living apart. This surprised no one, but their decision to marry soon after astonished everyone. As it turned out, Wollstonecraft was pregnant and unwilling to bear another child out of wedlock. To his friends Godwin explained that morality "is nothing but a balance between opposite evils."

Domestic life must not have been as bad as Godwin once imagined. When Wollstonecraft died a few months after bearing their daughter, Godwin remarried. More lessons in the practical applications of his theories were to come.

Family and parenthood were two of the evils he wanted to stamp out, but he now found himself utterly charmed by his daughter, Mary. She was just sixteen when the twenty-two-year-old poet Percy Shelley sought refuge from his debtors by knocking on Godwin's door. At the time, Shelley was not only famous for his poems but also for his radicalism, and Godwin's book had been like a candle in the darkness to him. Godwin opened up his home. To his horror his daughter soon opened up her heart.

Shelley was married and already a father. Godwin denounced the "licentious love" between the older married man and his young daughter, and threatened legal action. Shelley said he would give up Mary, and left the house. Soon he was back, waving a gun and a bottle of laudanum, and threatening to enter into a suicide pact with Mary. A few days later Shelley and Mary ran off—and took with them Godwin's stepchild, Jane, by his second wife.

Now things turned into a full-scale soap opera. Shelley proposed a ménage à trois with Mary to his wife, who was pregnant with his second child. Thrown out of the house, Shelley, Mary, and Jane proceeded to live and travel together. Godwin refused to see any of them, all the while continually badgering Shelley for money, which he sent. At some point, Jane changed her name to Claire and commenced an independent affair with Lord Byron, by whom she had a child. Meanwhile, Shelley also managed to seduce Mary Wollstonecraft's first daughter, Fanny, and out of unrequited love she committed suicide. If this wasn't enough, his wife, Harriet, a month later also committed suicide. A month after *that* Shelley and Mary married, much to Godwin's relief. Two years into their marriage Shelley began an affair with Claire (once Jane), who gave birth to Shelley's child, prompting Mary to retaliate with a novel—unpublished until after her death—about incest, which Godwin found "disgusting and detestable." (She also wrote *Frankenstein*, perhaps to convey how terribly wrong theoretical experiments can go.)

With all this wreckage around him, Shelley had the good sense to die at the age of twenty-nine in 1822. Godwin outlived his ardent disciple by fourteen years, enough time to reflect on both the public and private ravages of his theorizing. Not only did the French Revolution end in the twin evils of the Reign of Terror and Napoleon (as Burke had predicted it would), but his beloved daughter's happiness had been sacrificed on the altar of his ideas.

By the end of his life Godwin repudiated most of those ideas, becoming a defender of religion and the Whig party and decrying in his last book "the philosopher in his closet" who invents "imaginary schemes of policy" without any understanding of the necessary preconditions that make life livable. One really doesn't have to wonder whom he had in mind.

▶ Remember: Before you set out to remake your organization according to some grand theory, think through the consequences. As brilliant as you may be, things usually exist the way they do for a reason. Upheaval can lead to disaster.

The Murder That Shook a Kingdom

Be sure of the tone you set

To understand any organization, look to the top. A pushy, demanding boss will create a pushy, demanding culture. A legalistic, bureaucratic boss will rule over a company of would-be attorneys who niggle and nag but don't accomplish much. A positive leader will create a can-do atmosphere. The tone comes from the top.

Peter Drucker tells a story that shows how a leader sets the priorities and values for an entire organization. On the morning after the great New York power blackout of 1965, only one New York newspaper managed to get an edition on the streets, the *New York Times*. Executives had managed to locate a printing plant in New Jersey that could handle their million-copy press run but only in the ninety minutes scheduled for downtime. But when the *Times* run was finished, less than five hundred thousand copies actually made it off the press. At the last minute the entire edition had been held up when the editor spotted a wrongly hyphenated word on the front page. The editor and his subordinates argued over *this one word* for forty-eight minutes—half the available press time. Asked later if he had made the right decision, the editor said he was not going to let the *New York Times'* hundred-year-old reputation for accuracy be damaged by a mere power outage.

The story of one editor's devotion to the *Times'* high standards has become legendary in publishing circles. Other leaders have been less high-minded, and set examples that have come back to haunt them.

In 1513 Niccolò Machiavelli wrote *The Prince*, which was to become one of the most influential books ever published. Machiavelli argued that a ruler was not bound by ethics or morals but should only be concerned with acquiring power and achieving success. He sought through historical examples to uncover the precepts by which a ruler could impose his will on his subjects and opponents. One of his favorite illustrations was the career of Ferdinand, king of Aragon, a ruler so ruthless that Machiavelli nominated him as his perfect prince.

Ferdinand's great-grandson became Philip II of Spain, and he took Machiavelli's lesson to heart. Machiavellian to the core, Philip followed wholeheartedly the Italian's dictum that the end justifies the means, and that his private morality—Philip was a devout Catholic—had nothing whatsoever to do with his public actions. As a result, he was portrayed as a hero at home and a tyrant everywhere else. He persecuted Protestants in the Netherlands, executed Flemish reformers, tried to undermine Elizabeth of England, sent the ill-fated Armada against her, and conspired in the assassination of Holland's founding father, William the Silent.

He single-handedly ruled an empire that extended from the Philippines, which he named after himself, to the Americas. He relished the fear he inspired, just as Machiavelli had advised. However, he was at the same time instilling his philosophy in his own subordinates, a consequence Machiavelli seems never to have considered. His courtiers became as ruthless as their king.

In the early part of his reign Philip embraced one courtier as a close political confidant, ennobling him as prince of Eboli and duke of Pastrana and marrying him to the greatest heiress in Spain, Ana de Mendoza. When the Prince of Eboli died in 1573, Philip advanced his private secretary, one Antonio Pérez, to the position the prince had occupied close to the throne. The king took the widowed princess of Eboli to be his mistress. Interestingly, the princess and Pérez may have already been lovers, a complication which would later compound their misery.

Philip had an illegitimate half-brother, Don Juan of Austria, the fruit of his father Charles V's fling with an innkeeper's daughter. Don Juan was the flamboyant commander of the allied fleets that had crushed the Ottoman navy in 1571; as a result he was the hero of Christendom. Eventually he persuaded Philip to appoint him governor of the Netherlands. To keep the headstrong Don Juan in line, the king and Pérez arranged for one of Pérez' protégés, Juan de Escobedo, to be sent along as private secretary to the new governor. Once installed in the Netherlands, Don Juan quickly developed his own ideas of how the territory should be governed, ideas that were frowned upon in Madrid. Exasperated because his policies were misunderstood, Don Juan sent Escobedo to explain them to Philip.

On arriving in Madrid, Escobedo realized that Pérez was actually the one undermining Don Juan's position. He immediately— and unwisely—denounced the king's favorite. Pérez countered and tried to convince Philip that Escobedo was encouraging Don Juan's vanity and greed. Between them, Philip and Pérez agreed the situation could best be contained if Escobedo were done away with—a task left to Pérez.

Escobedo was assassinated in March 1578 by hired ruffians in a Madrid street, but not without a struggle or witnesses whose cries woke up the town. The next day the entire city was talking about the sensational murder that led back to Pérez and the king.

Philip had not foreseen this public relations catastrophe. When a member of the royal council demanded an inquiry, he clumsily tried to protect Pérez but the scandal continued to simmer. Don Juan died in October, and his private papers arrived in Madrid the following spring. They revealed Pérez' duplicity and Escobedo's innocence. Pérez maneuvered desperately to avert being nailed as the fall guy, but the murmuring now implicated the king himself, and Philip had to act. In July 1579 both Pérez and the princess of Eboli were arrested.

Less than a year later, Pérez escaped from prison and fled to Zaragoza in Aragon, where by ancient right he could evade the king's warrant. Philip was temporarily stymied. He ordered the Holy Office to help him, and soon Pérez was incarcerated on a trumped-up charge of heresy. Political tension was so high in Aragon's capital city, however, that rioting broke out shortly afterward, and a mob stormed the inquisitorial headquarters and freed Pérez. Taking no further chances, Pérez rode hard for the French border.

Philip's vengeance fell upon his mistress instead. The princess of Eboli was banished from court and condemned to live the rest of her life in the upstairs salon of her palace at Pastrana in the Castilian mountains—with the great window walled up to block its magnificent view. Today, the palace of Pastrana is still there. And in Madrid the locals still dine in the tavern in front of which Escobedo bled to death on the pavement.

True to his teacher Machiavelli, Philip knew something must be done to divert the public's attention from the domestic crisis he and his courtiers had caused. A few months later he invaded Portugal.

▶ Remember: A leader's attitudes are reflected not in words but in deeds. Always be aware of what your actions tell your subordinates about your values.

The Legend of Prester John

Base no plans on hope

Informed that a friend who had endured an unhappy marriage had recently wed again, Samuel Johnson remarked, "It's a triumph of hope over experience."

"Hope is a good breakfast," wrote Francis Bacon, "but it is a bad supper." Indeed, many of life's disappointments have their roots in our own minds. Humans necessarily operate with limited information: we simply don't know everything. Because our information is full of gaps, we fill them in with our hopes. With those gaps filled, we look down the road to the future as if it were level and smooth. Instead it is full of large potholes covered up by our imaginations.

In twelfth-century Europe an entire society allowed itself to be deluded by hope. Prester John was a cloudy figure, thought to be a prince of some faraway Christian nation in the East. Somehow the idea arose that this great prince was on his way to accomplish Christendom's most cherished dream—the liberation of the Holy Land.

The legend of Prester John, and the disastrous effects that were to flow from it, had its origins in two unrelated historical events, separated by centuries.

In the fifth century a patriarch of Constantinople—Nestorius—was deposed when he began to preach that Jesus was merely a man infused with the Holy Spirit and that the Virgin Mary was therefore not "the Mother of God." He and his followers were exiled, and they seem to have made their way eastward. We know his version of Christianity spread to India, and from there made its way to China, where it may have found fertile ground in regions heavily influence by Buddhism. In 1122 an Indian priest appeared at the papal court claiming to be an envoy of the Nestorian Christians of India. In 1145 the pope received a letter from a bishop in Syria reporting rumors that a Christian prince in the Far East did indeed exist and was preparing to send an army to wrest

Jerusalem from the Muslims. The purported army never arrived, so the next pope sent a delegation to track down the prince. The delegation never returned. But the rumors persisted, and somehow this mighty Christian prince even gained a name: Prester John.

The second event occurred in 1218, and Christian Europe knew nothing about it.

In that year a caravan of five hundred camels arrived at the border of Muslim Samarkand, north of Persia near the Aral Sea, laden with silk, sables, gold, and silver. The strangers said they came from a distant land and wished to open a trade route. The provincial governor at the border thought he knew a good thing when he saw it. He murdered the infidels and confiscated their treasure. Soon an indignant delegation arrived at the court of Ala al-Din Muhammad Shah, ruler of Samarkand. The foreign ambassador protested that an act of goodwill had been despoiled. On behalf of his ruler, he demanded restitution. Instead of reprimanding his governor, the shah arrogantly ordered the foreign ambassador's head cut off, then gave it to the surviving foreigners to take it back to wherever they had come from. This was to be a mistake the whole world would soon regret.

The murdered ambassador's prince three years before had completed his partial conquest of North China. He was not pleased by the insult delivered by the Muslim shah.

Within months the shah and his kingdom were under the assault of the most ferocious and effective army that had ever marched. In 1221 the bishop of Acre in Palestine wrote urgently to the pope that a Christian prince had destroyed a huge Muslim empire to the east and was now sweeping through Persia. The news elated Christian Europe, and the pope hastily called for new armies to be raised across the continent to renew the Fifth Crusade and give aid to this Christian prince in retaking the Holy Land.

The pope had made a crucial error. He launched a new offensive just when he should have been organizing Christian rulers for Europe's defense.

The name Prester John must have passed through many languages, from Mongol to Chinese to Turkish to Persian to Syrian to

Greek and finally to Latin. Even in English it bears a striking resemblance to the name of the ruler who descended with such anger on the hapless Muslims and who soon turned his attention to Christian Europe itself.

Amazed by the wealth of the new lands they conquered and fired by reports of even greater riches in the West, the Mongol hordes razed everything in their path. The great leader they served was to be known as "the punishment of God." To history he is known as Genghis Khan.

▶ Remember: Your hopes are not reality. Counting on them can lead to strategic mistakes—and even devastation.

The Mistake That Split the World

Don't rely on the rule book

A good coach knows how to follow the playbook. A great coach knows when to ignore it. Whether capitalizing on an opponent's weakness or riding a wave of team momentum, the great rise above the merely good by knowing when to take risks.

Military leaders are drilled in tactics and strategy, but in the fog of war it's hard to know where one's left flank is, much less what it's doing; the playbook is not so much thrown away as blown away. Military theory is just that—theory. As Mike Tyson once put it, "Everyone has a game plan until he's hit in the mouth."

T. E. Lawrence was an archaeology student when World War I broke out. Because he had learned Arabic on digging expeditions, he was assigned to British Military Intelligence in Cairo. After a year or so Lawrence was attached to Arab forces fighting against the Turks. The Turkish stronghold was Aqaba on the Red Sea, an inlet so well defended by massive artillery that the British were

loath to attack it. The only other approach was across a treacherous stretch of desert known as the Sun's Anvil. Lawrence was so
ignorant of military tactics that he didn't know this approach was
impossible; all he knew was that his Arabs and their camels were
good at crossing deserts. So he attacked Aqaba from the rear, and
took it—turning himself overnight into a national hero.

If the Byzantine emperor Alexius in 1096 had been as ignorant of military theory as Lawrence, the schism between Eastern
and Western Christianity might never have happened.

Traditionally, the Great Schism of the Eastern and Western
churches is thought to date from 1054, when a theological dispute
over the Nicene Creed led the Orthodox churches to break deci-
sively with Rome. But it's unlikely that the great powers of the time
were all that concerned about a theological dispute. And recent evidence shows that even the theologians didn't intend a break. Twenty
years after the so-called split a new pope in Rome didn't even know
it had occurred. As is so often the case, history textbooks look for
dates, not causes. There was one cause, and it wasn't theology.
Rather it was an emperor's decision to stick with the rule book.

Alexius ruled the Byzantine Empire, but he considered himself the Roman emperor. His was the inheritance of Constantine,
founder of Constantinople. His Greek-speaking people called
themselves *Rhomaioi* and thought of their empire as *Romania*.
They considered the West its subject as much as the East, and
from time to time made excursions against the barbarian tribes in
Italy or extracted tribute from their kings to prove the point. Although this vestige of the ancient Roman Empire would last until
1453, by the eleventh century it was already under serious threat
from invading Turks under the banner of Islam.

Emperor Alexius was a capable military officer, well trained in
Roman strategy and tactics, who had won the crown in an army
coup d'état (a way to the throne not unknown in Rome). The
army had revolted in alarm over the Turks' encroachment into
Asia Minor and their capture of rich lands that produced the
army's food, not to mention most of its soldiers. On taking the
throne, Alexius recognized that the situation was deteriorating,
and that he needed help.

In 1095 he sent ambassadors to appeal to Pope Urban II, and after a few months of diplomacy the pope suddenly announced a great crusade to liberate Eastern Christianity from the depredations of Islam. Although Alexius needed help, he wasn't sure he wanted that much help, and his worst fears were confirmed in the summer of 1096 when the first of five great armies, totaling perhaps eighty thousand warriors and camp followers, began descending on Constantinople.

Alexius was well acquainted with Western feudal customs, which he immediately exploited to make sure this great army worked for him and not against him. He had the nobles leading the Christian army swear homage to him as their liege lord. He would provide food, supplies, and logistical support. As his vassals, the Westerners would be honor-bound to defend him, and he would be honor-bound to protect them.

By early June, the Crusader army had cut a swath through Asia Minor and, after a long and arduous siege, recaptured Antioch in Syria, once the capital of Roman Asia. The Turks quickly recovered from this disaster, encircling Antioch and raising a new and greater army to retake it.

News of the victory overjoyed Alexius, but the even fresher news about a new Muslim army left him in a quandary. If his well-trained Imperial regulars relieved the Crusaders at Antioch, they and the Crusaders could then march farther south, perhaps even retaking Jerusalem, which had sporadically been under Constantinople's rule. But if the new Muslim army defeated his troops and the Crusaders, the entire peninsula would be unprotected and Constantinople itself endangered. What was he to do? Keep his feudal obligation to the Crusaders, march to their defense, and hope for a decisive victory? Or follow classic Roman military doctrine, hold his assets in reserve, and protect his capital? Alexius stopped where he was, set his troops up in a defensive perimeter, proceeded back to Constantinople, and awaited events. He knew his military science, and he followed what he knew. It was the only prudent thing to do.

The Crusaders, not surprisingly, didn't see it that way. When they miraculously defeated the great Muslim army at Antioch and marched on alone to Jerusalem (which they took, improbably enough, in July 1099), they reviled Alexius as a traitor to his feudal oath and to the cause of Christendom. With the angry blessing of the pope, the Crusaders established their own string of Western Christian states from Antioch to the Arabian Desert, as fiercely hostile to Constantinople as they were to Islam. European public opinion swung heavily against any remaining claim of the Byzantine Empire to its Roman pretensions, deriding its rulers as "deceitful and treacherous Greeks."

The heritage of Rome was torn in two, and Christianity along with it. Constantinople was fatally weakened, all the Middle East was eventually lost to Islam, and the West and East were locked in permanent suspicion of each other. All because a capable man was too prudent to be a great one.

▶ **Remember: The conventional doctrines don't always apply. Alexius played it safe and followed the rules. If he had broken the rules he could have broken the back of the Muslim army and reestablished Roman rule over the known world. When the situation calls for it, make your own rules.**

The Little Flower of St. Francis

Lead by example

One morning after the German occupation, Denmark's King Christian spotted a Nazi flag flying over a public building. He called the German commander and ordered the flag taken down. The German refused. The king said he would have a soldier take it down. The German said he would have the soldier shot. "I think not," replied the seventy-three-year-old king, "because I will be the soldier." The flag came down.

A few months later the Germans ordered all Jews in Denmark, beginning on a certain day, to wear a yellow armband so they could be easily picked out. The morning the order took effect, the king emerged from the palace grounds for his daily horseback ride wearing a yellow armband. By afternoon, yellow armbands were the most popular item for sale in the country.

To get rid of this troublesome old man, Hitler ordered him imprisoned. That was the last straw for a Danish people who had wanted no part in the war. In the early morning hours the day after their king's arrest was announced, thousands of men slipped out of their homes and villages, made their way to the coasts, and launched hundreds of fishing boats and small skiffs to England to join the Allied armies. "Suddenly one morning, the sea wasn't full of gulls, it was full of Danes," said a British naval captain.

The Danish king had never delivered a stirring word. He had never made an impassioned speech. He never reprimanded anyone for collaborating with the enemy. He simply resisted.

The power of leading by example is shown by an incident in the history of one of the world's oldest continually functioning organizations, the Franciscans.

After his conversation in 1205 St. Francis of Assisi became known as a dazzling and effective preacher, but he didn't inspire a spiritual revolution with words. He lived his idea more than he preached it. The simplicity of this bold new concept—that instead of talking about Christ one should try living like Him—brought Francis international notoriety and hordes of followers.

He attracted so many followers that they became a problem, because these enthusiastic seekers had to be organized, taught, fed, clothed, and managed. Before long, Francis' simple message was subsumed into the task of organizing his followers to get the message out. Francis himself finally rebelled against this systemization, and he spent the last seven years of his ministry in virtual spiritual retreat.

Bernard of Quintavalle was one of Francis' first disciples, and he too worried that Francis' simple and joyous ascetic vision would be undermined by the inevitable entropy that infects all institutions. He decided to do something about it, not by warning his brothers in the order, or chiding them, or arguing with them, but by showing them the way.

He decided to convert the city of Bologna. This target was particularly challenging: it was a rich town on the road between Rome and Venice, and had for half a century been home to the greatest law school in medieval Christianity. Not too many lawyers have ever been overly fond of poverty, and most have instinctively preferred system to inspiration.

The story of Bernard's mission to Bologna is told in *The Little Flowers of St. Francis* as a lesson to all the friars who would come after him. The story begins with Bernard's entry into the city.

> When the children saw him in a ragged, shabby habit, they jeered at him and abused him, thinking him a madman. But Brother Bernard bore all this patiently and gladly for the love of Christ. And in order to receive even worse treatment, he sat down openly in the marketplace of the city. As he sat there a crowd of children and men gathered round him: one tugged at his cowl from behind, and another from in front; one threw dust at him, and another stones; one pushed him in this direction, and another in that. But Brother Bernard remained patient and unruffled, neither complaining nor moving away. And for several days he returned to the same place to endure similar treatment.
>
> Since patience is evidence of perfection and proof of virtue, a wise doctor of law, seeing Brother Bernard's great constancy and virtue, and considering how he remained undaunted by any ill-treatment and mockery during all these days, said to himself: "It is impossible that this is not a holy man." And coming up to him, he asked, "Who are you, and why have you come here?"
>
> In reply Brother Bernard put his hand into his breast, and drawing out the Rule of Saint Francis, gave it to him to read. When he had read it and recognized its sublime counsel of perfection, he turned to his friends with the greatest wonder and admiration, saying: "This is assuredly the highest form of the religious life of which I have ever heard. This man and his companions are the holiest men in the world, and whoever abuses them is the greatest of sinners, for he is the true friend of God and deserves the highest honor."

And he said to Brother Bernard, "If you need a place where you can serve God in a fitting manner, I will gladly provide it for the salvation of my soul."

Brother Bernard answered: "Sir, I believe that Our Lord Jesus Christ has inspired you to make this offer, and I gladly accept it for the honor of Christ."

So the judge led Brother Bernard to his house with great joy and affection, and gave him the promised house, which he prepared and furnished at his own expense. And thenceforward he acted like a father to him, and was the foremost protector of Brother Bernard and his companions.

Because of the holiness of his life, Brother Bernard began to be revered by all the people, so that any who could see or touch him counted himself blessed. But, as a disciple of Christ and of the humble Saint Francis, Bernard feared lest the respect of this world might impede the peace and salvation of his soul. So he left the town and returned to Saint Francis, saying: "Father, the friary has been established in Bologna. So send friars to occupy and maintain it, for I can do no good there; indeed, I fear to lose more than I could gain because of the excessive respect paid to me."

When St. Francis had received a full account of all that God had done through Brother Bernard, he gave thanks to Him who had begun to increase the poor little disciples of the Cross in this manner. And he sent some of his companions to Bologna and into Lombardy, where they established many friaries in various places.

By the time these words were written (ca. 1320), the Franciscan order had become a mighty corporation with a complex constitution, great wealth, hundreds of schools and convents, and thousands of friars and sisters from Morocco to the Mongol Empire. But unlike many other orders founded before and after it, the Franciscans never lost their sense of purpose, regained for them by the simple action of a brother who took St. Francis seriously enough to imitate him.

▶ **Remember: St. Bernard's example revived the mission of an organization that has flourished for six hundred years. What kind** of example do you set for the people you want to lead? Would your second-in-command do as well as Bernard in reawakening in your organization your original values and goals?

What the Milkmaids Knew

Trust the wisdom of people who work with their hands

One of the curiosities of the modern world is that our most highly trained experts—scientists, executives, engineers, and the like—often seem inept when confronted with any problem outside the narrow boundaries of their expertise. In some ways this is partly due to the training itself. They become accustomed to the rigor and preciseness of the laboratory, to the routine and predictability of the office, to the scholarly isolation of the library. They lose the survival skills—if they ever had them—of the rougher and humbler sorts of laborers who must deal daily with the vagaries of nature, the whims of bosses, the unpredictability of markets, and the intrusions of fools. For these reasons, the humbler jobs seem to produce the people most capable of dealing with the exigencies of life. The delusions that sometimes afflict business executives, philosophers, and even first-rate scientists are rare among fishermen, farmers, and sailors. These are people who are very careful not to deceive themselves for the simple reason that mistakes are often fatal. As a result, they have a wisdom that is made up of equal parts prudence, flexibility, perseverance, and resignation. And for that reason, it is often sensible to listen to them.

Just after the Nazi invasion of Poland, *Time* magazine founder Henry Luce wandered into an open-air market in Rome. In his conversations with upper-class Italians, Luce had detected growing discontent with the seventeen-year-old Fascist regime and distrust of Germany's intentions. As a way of testing the climate of opinion among the common people, he asked an old fruit vendor the question everyone seemed to be talking about, Could Italy manage to stay out of the war? The old man looked up at him with weary eyes. "No, sir," he said. "This is a war that must be fought, because this is a war that must be lost." In all his conversations with the great and the mighty, Luce later recounted, he had never received an answer steeped in such simple wisdom.

Or as William F. Buckley, Jr., once wrote, he would rather be governed by the first two hundred people in the Boston telephone directory than by the entire faculty of Harvard College.

The modern tendency to trust in experts began with the Enlightenment on the one hand and the concurrent rise of the scientific method on the other. If the accumulated wisdom of the ages wasn't to be valued anymore, how much could common folk wisdom be worth? Along with folk wisdom went folk medicine, which was dismissed as hokum by the newly enthroned scientific establishment.

In isolated cases, though, a few doctors retained a native curiosity about why the old ways seemed to work. William Withering wondered why local folk healers prescribed the leaves of the common foxglove as an antidote to chest pains; by 1785 he had confirmed that properties of the foxglove (of the genus *Digitalis*) prevented heart disease, and today digitalis is the most commonly prescribed antidote for heart problems. Likewise, James Lind, a surgeon in the Royal Navy, listened when old seamen told him lemons and limes bring about good luck on ships; he published his study of vitamin C deficiency in *A Treatise on the Scurvy* in 1753, leading the Admiralty to require lemon juice aboard every warship. Withering and Lind, like publisher Luce, were following the advice of Ptahhotep the Egyptian, who forty-eight centuries earlier advised, "Do not be arrogant because of your knowledge, but confer with the ignorant man as well as the learned."

Withering and Lind weren't the only ones to pay attention to the common wisdom of their day and to link a pattern to the larger chain of cause and effect. Darwin is said to have first become intrigued with the theory of natural selection by noting how farmers bred their animals to produce better strains in their livestock.

The battle that ended smallpox had its beginning in a bit of folk wisdom. It started with an overheard remark.

Nobody alive today can imagine how horrible a scourge smallpox was in the centuries before us. Voltaire estimated that out of every hundred people, sixty contracted the disease, and of those, twenty died. French monasteries and nunneries were estimated to contain two hundred thousand sufferers from the disease, who because of their disfigurement had withdrawn from the world. By 1977 the United Nations declared that smallpox had finally been eliminated (but to show how deadly it can be, a clinician working on a sample in 1979 accidentally touched the virus and died).

In 1763, at the customary age of fourteen, Edward Jenner was apprenticed to a doctor near his home in Gloucestershire, England, in preparation for his entering the medical profession. One day during his apprenticeship, Jenner overheard a young milkmaid contradict the doctor when he mentioned that she might be coming down with smallpox. That wasn't possible, the girl replied, because she already had a cowpox sore on her hand, and everyone knew that once you had cowpox you never got smallpox. The doctor shrugged off the remark, but Jenner was intrigued. How did "everyone" know what the milkmaid stated so confidently, when medicine had no clue how to prevent smallpox?

Hard as it is for the modern mind to grasp, as late as the American Civil War the idea of infection was largely unknown in the Western world. More soldiers in that great conflict, for example, died from the infected instruments used to treat their wounds than from the wounds themselves.

As Jenner grew to maturity and came into his own practice, he continued to fight smallpox with the few tools available to him, but he never forgot the milkmaid's claim. Cowpox seemed to be a common condition of the cattle in the shire, but it was such a milder version of the smallpox disease infecting humans that it seemed not to bother the cows at all. And those humans who were exposed to cowpox only seemed to develop a few sores at the point of contact, usually on their hands, which quickly disappeared on their own. When he had an off moment or a free afternoon, he would wander over to the farms scattered around the countryside and watch the milkmaids ply their trade. He kept note of their unblemished skin, especially in contrast to the scars of their neighbors. He tried to understand how they contracted cowpox and how that related to the spread of smallpox. He had firmly come to believe that the folk wisdom relayed by the milkmaid years ago contained a truth he hadn't yet grasped.

On May 14, 1796—nearly thirty years after the remark that had puzzled him and after decades of watching some people contract the disease while others seemed immune to it, but still with no general understanding of infectious disease to propel him forward—Jenner decided to risk an experiment. That afternoon a young girl by the name of Sarah Nelmes, a milkmaid, came to him complaining of a cowpox pustule. He took a tissue sample from the sore and with it inoculated the arm of James Phipps, a boy of eight in good health. The inoculation produced disease in James, as expected. But Jenner noted that while its sores progressed in much the same way as smallpox, the successive stages were much milder. Twenty days later, when James was fully recovered from his bout of cowpox, Jenner took his greatest gamble. He inoculated the boy with straight smallpox. The diseased material had no effect.

The concept of vaccination had been discovered. In the next two hundred years it would be responsible for the eradication of not only smallpox, but of polio, diphtheria, whooping cough, and many other life-threatening diseases.

The source of Jenner's great discovery is unlikely ever to be forgotten, not because we remember our heroes but because we rely on words. "Vaccination" comes from the Latin *vaccinus*—"of cows."

▶ Remember: Great things can come out of the laboratory, but wisdom most often comes from the land. Don't let your education or training make you feel so superior that you aren't open to the ideas of those ostensibly beneath you. A leader is someone who is always ready to be taught.

part seven

BEING YOUR PERSONAL BEST

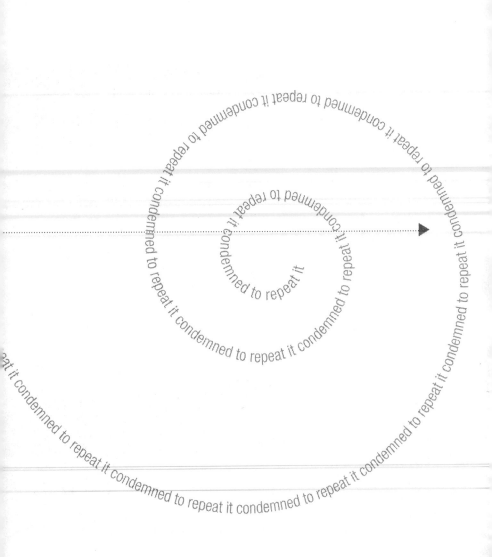

Why Sir Walter Raleigh Lost His Head

Rely on grit, not grease

At one time George Orwell was under contract to write an adventure serial for a boy's weekly magazine. The formula for these serials, like those films in the old Saturday matinees, was fairly rigid. By the end of each installment the hero had to have gotten into such a dangerous and seemingly impossible fix that everyone would buy next week's magazine to see how he got out of it. When working on one of these installments, Orwell wrote his hero into a situation so impossible that Orwell himself was now in a fix. He struggled for days and as the deadline got nearer and nearer, he was still working on some way to save his young protagonist. Finally a waiting copyboy grabbed the manuscript from his hands, crossed out the first paragraph, instead wrote, "With one bound Jack was free," and rushed it off to the typesetters.

The copyboy could solve the problem when Orwell couldn't because the copyboy was just that—a boy. For him the solution was effortless because he didn't yet know much about effort. Orwell couldn't see the easy solution because his experience had taught him that solutions aren't easy. But there are always those who believe they are, and not all of them are boys.

Sir Walter Raleigh's exploits in the late 1560s had taken him to France, America, and Ireland before he made his entry at Elizabeth's court—and what an entry it was. The incident is first recorded nearly a hundred years after the fact in Thomas Fuller's *Worthies of England,* published in 1662: "The captain Raleigh coming out of Ireland to the English court . . . found the queen walking, till meeting with a plashy place, she seemed to scruple going thereon. Presently Raleigh cast and spread his new plush cloak on the ground, whereon the queen trod gently, rewarding him later with many suits, for his so free and seasonable tender of so fair a footcloth. Thus an advantageous admission into the first notice of a prince is more than half a degree to preferment."

Raleigh made the most of it. A few days later he wrote in the dust of a windowpane near where the queen liked to sit, "Fain would I climb, yet fear I to fall," under which Elizabeth herself wrote, "If thy heart fails thee, climb not at all."

Raleigh proved to be the perfect courtier, entertaining the queen with his wit and charm, and basking in her favor. Elizabeth enjoyed playing the hen pampered by her gallant roosters, but Raleigh equally enjoyed being a rooster amid all the hens of the royal household. When one of his seductions produced a child, Elizabeth's jealousy was inflamed, but this seemed only to work in his favor. She showered him with gifts and offices, appointed him to her personal guard, and all in all made him a very rich man.

Such favors with so little accomplishment behind them gained Raleigh powerful enemies, mainly among those whose work kept the kingdom running. Raleigh, restless by nature, was also smart enough to realize that he needed to make his mark. He persuaded Elizabeth to grant him a patent to chart undiscovered lands in the Americas. He explored the North American seaboard from Newfoundland to Florida, and named Virginia for his virgin queen. Tradition holds that Raleigh imported tobacco and potatoes from the New World to the Old. (The story of Sir Walter's servant, approaching from behind Raleigh's high-backed chair and, seeing smoke billowing upward, dousing him with water, is probably apocryphal.)

But for all the time and effort invested in his voyages, they brought him little profit and even less gratitude from a sovereign who measured accomplishment in cold, hard cash. In 1592 the queen caught him *in flagrante delicto* with Elizabeth Throgmorton, another lady-in-waiting. Tiring of this foolishness, she sent him to the Tower of London. When Raleigh was released, he compounded his offense by promptly marrying the lady, which added fire to the queen's indignation. Elizabeth banished him from court.

But Raleigh was still looking for the one big play that would put him over the top. The legendary treasure city of Manoa would be his ticket, he decided, and he managed to talk Elizabeth into financing a voyage to discover the "lost city." A few months later, he returned from the Spanish Main with a few lumps of quartz speckled with gold. One good thing did come out of the failure, however: his *Discovery of the Empyre of Guiana* (1596) marks him among the finest writers of so fertile an age in literature. But Raleigh was too restless to stick to the one thing in which he actually showed talent. To regain Elizabeth's favor he signed on to fight against the Spanish.

His fortunes, however, sank fast with the death of Elizabeth in 1603 and the accession of James I, son of Mary, Queen of Scots. Raleigh had dabbled too often in dangerous political schemes, and the new king suspected the adventurer had played a part in his mother's execution. Raleigh found himself arrested, sent to the Tower on charges of high treason, tried, found guilty, and condemned to death. His few friends at court prevailed upon the new king, and the sentence was commuted to life imprisonment.

But Raleigh wasn't through. He plotted, cajoled, and conjured up new schemes out of thin air—and finally in 1616 James allowed him one last chance. This time Raleigh was convinced that an expedition up the Orinoco would find gold, and he offered to pay the expenses himself. The king's permission was granted on one condition: Raleigh must not take any hostile acts against the Spanish, whose long-standing enmity the king was working to soothe. At the mouth of the river, Raleigh fell ill. He delegated the exploration to a trusted lieutenant, who not only found no gold but got embroiled in a battle with the Spanish at San Tomás and burned the town. Raleigh tried to talk his men into trying again, but they understandably valued their lives more than his dreams. Forced to return to England empty-handed, Raleigh may have known his time was up. As it was, news of the San Tomás raid made it to England before he did, and the Spanish ambassador had already complained vociferously to the king. Raleigh was arrested upon landing. He was beheaded on October 29, 1618, in front of a great London crowd that was amazed at the amount of blood that could flow from a body over sixty years old.

John Aubrey wrote a gracious epitaph, saying Raleigh "had many things to be commended for in his life, but none more than his constancy at his death, which he tooke with so undaunted a resolution that one might perceive that he had a certain expectation of a better life after it." If so, it was the one constant thing Raleigh ever did.

▶ Remember: A famous life doesn't necessarily mean a useful one. Raleigh's type is always near—charming, persuasive, full of big talk about the next big deal. Keep at your work. Jack may have with one bound set himself free, but success is achieved by small steps up a steep hill, one at a time.

The Dumb Ox Who Remade the World

Practice humility

When he was president of Israel in the early 1950s, Chaim Weizmann boarded a ship to Europe and was delighted to discover Einstein as a fellow passenger. After two hours with him, Weizmann said, "I felt I not only understood the theory of relativity but I was pretty well pleased with myself for having invented it." (After the ship had docked and the passengers had made their farewells, Mrs. Weizmann remarked to her husband that he didn't look well. "How can I after what Einstein just said to me?" She asked what Einstein had said. "He looked at me, and said, 'Be good.' ")

All achievers have healthy egos. But the truly great achievers share one notable characteristic: they are humble. "I do not know what I may appear to the world," wrote Newton, "but to myself I seem to have been only like a boy playing on the seashore, and diverting myself in now and then finding a smoother pebble or a prettier shell than ordinary, whilst the great ocean of truth lay undiscovered before me."

Thomas Aquinas was so shy, quiet, slow, and overweight that he was mocked by his fellow students as the "dumb ox." On hearing some of his pupils deriding Aquinas with that name, their teacher, Albert the Great, remarked, "Yes, and his lowing will be heard throughout the world."

In a time of intellectual upheaval Aquinas undertook the systematic defense of Christianity on every front, marshaling arguments like armies and sending them out to crush all opposition. He drew from everyone—Aristotle, the Muslim thinker Averroës, the great Jewish rabbi Maimonides—and enlisted them in his ranks.

He was made Christian Europe's youngest master of theology at the age of thirty-four by direct intervention of the pope. And he had only just begun. He formulated the now-classic distinction between *theology* (the study of revealed doctrine) and *philosophy* (the study of data derived from reasoned investigation), and dedicated his considerable energies to identifying the territory both these "sciences" could profitably explore. In doing so he became the champion of the tradition in Western thought that sees no final contradiction between hard reason and deep faith. His great *Summa Theologica* contains not just every argument for Christianity but every argument he could muster *against* it, a veritable handbook for the village atheist.

Despite the awe with which he was held by his contemporaries, Aquinas seemed to regard himself more as a vessel of ideas than as the creator of them. He followed the same routine as any other friar, attended all the hours of prayer, said or heard Mass every day, taught to earn his living, and remained unmoved by the world's acclaim. As one historian remarked, "His writings span the universe but contain not one immodest word."

A great duke once insisted on meeting the famous theologian while he was living at the St. Jacques convent in Paris. The duke wanted the honor of doing something generous for the renowned thinker, for the Dominican order, for *somebody*. The two were walking along the banks of the Seine as the duke made his insistent offer, so Aquinas stopped and pointed to a stall where caged birds were being sold. Buy all those, the friar requested. Eager to comply, the duke did as he was bidden. When all the cages were piled in front of the scholar, Aquinas with delight bent down and opened every one. Depriving a winged creature of its ability to fly struck his logical Aristotelian mind as an atrocity.

One day while standing with some students in Montmartre overlooking Paris, one of the young men exclaimed, "Paris should belong to you." Aquinas asked in reply, "And what would I do with it?" "Sell it to the king of France, and then you'd have all the money you need for whatever you wanted!" "To tell you the truth," answered Aquinas, "right now I'd rather have the commentary of St. John Chrysostom on St. Matthew's gospel."

Like many great minds he was often intensely in conversation with himself. He was once invited to dine with Louis IX and during the course of the meal he withdrew into himself, lost in meditation. Suddenly he struck the table with his fist and exclaimed, "That is the decisive argument against the Manicheans." The other guests were appalled. "You are sitting at the table of the king of France," his prior reminded him. The king, however, was pleased that such a moment had occurred in his presence, and ordered an attendant to bring writing materials to the triumphant philosopher.

Near the end of his life the prodigious outflow suddenly stopped. He told a friend, "Such things have been revealed to me that what I have written seems but straw." When he died in 1274 his old mentor Albert the Great broke down in announcing the news, and finally said only, "He was the flower and glory of the world."

▶ Remember: Thomas Aquinas stands in a special class of intellect shared by Newton, Einstein, and few others. Yet even at that elevated height he remained in his own mind a lowly friar. Appraise yourself, and try to stay humble.

The Crown Lost by Lust

Keep yourself under control

John D. Rockefeller was once asked by a reporter how he chose his partners. "I look them in the eye," Rockefeller replied with a steely gaze. "If they don't flinch, they are my kind of men." The reporter didn't note whether he himself flinched.

When Thomas Edison set up his famous laboratory at Menlo Park, he received applications to join him from all over the world. Edison was intent on establishing an "invention factory," where teams of competent people could work on different aspects of an idea until the invention was complete. He hired mechanics and toolmakers, and finally even a mathematical physicist. The hardworking Edison, who, as one biographer noted, "was a genius who didn't believe in genius," had only one rule in selecting his employees: "they have to love to work harder than I do."

Rockefeller and Edison were notoriously driven men, and it's no surprise they expected the same from those who worked with them. But often leaders allow themselves to be seduced. Who can resist being told how brilliant they are, how farsighted, how powerful and wise? And who can resist hiring and promoting people who are smart enough to notice?

In many cases the modern CEO shows all the vanity of a peacock, with none of the color. Not that color matters. Mary, Queen of Scots, was about as colorful as they come, but she had a self-indulgent streak that would make the most preening CEOs blush. And one that should make them think.

When Mary Stuart was born in 1542 the chances were slim that she would even survive childhood, much less mount the throne. She was only six days old when her father, the king, died, leaving her as his only legitimate heir.

The nobles who controlled the throne were torn between pro-French/Catholic and pro-English/Protestant factions. Henry VIII of England began scheming for Mary's marriage to his son, the Prince of Wales, while she was still an infant. But Mary's French mother bitterly opposed this match, and when Edward died in his teens, Mary was sent to live in the French court. In 1558 at age sixteen, Mary was married to the French dauphin, François, but he died within a year. France then disowned the young widow, and she was shipped home in 1561.

Regally enthroned in Scotland, she now reigned at the age of nineteen as the first Scottish sovereign since her father's death. Contrary to many historical accounts, Mary proved to be a remarkably talented politician. She managed to balance the irreconcilable demands of the factions vying for control. As energetic as her beloved grandfather, James IV, she frequently traveled the countryside, charming her subjects and enchanting the contentious nobles.

The nation became embroiled with the question of whom she would marry. But Mary herself remained remarkably insouciant on such a large question; to her another arranged marriage meant another political performance. Better to choose her own lovers—and her own husbands—and keep them as powerless playthings. That might have worked (her cousin Elizabeth I proved good enough at the game) but for the intrigues of her court and her own weaknesses.

At the English court served a man named Henry Stewart, Lord Darnley, second in line to the Scottish throne. (Mary and Darnley had the same grandmother, Margaret Tudor.) For some reason—probably mischievous—Elizabeth sent Darnley home to

Scotland not long after Mary ascended the throne. At first sight of him, Mary became infatuated, calling him "the lustiest and best proportioned lang man ever to come her way." Darnley was empty-headed and temperamental, as Elizabeth undoubtedly knew, but Mary instantly decided to marry him. In 1565 he became Henry, King of Scots.

The marriage was bitterly unpopular, not to mention a disaster. Soon after the honeymoon, Darnley started flaunting his new status, only to find himself often overruled by his wife. Mary found it difficult to share the throne with a man who proved to be a dissolute, drunken debauchee. Unfortunately, Mary made fateful mistakes in trying to control him. She did not confide in men like her half-brother, the Earl of Moray, who had helped her when she first returned to Scotland. Instead, she turned to handsome, puffed-up courtiers like David Rizzio, her private secretary. This further infuriated Darnley, since he suspected Rizzio of being his wife's lover.

One March night in 1566, Darnley and a group of disaffected nobles broke into the queen's dining room when she was eating with Rizzio and stabbed the secretary to death. Mary was saved only by the fact that she was six months pregnant with Darnley's baby, Scotland's future monarch (who retained a lifelong fear of steel, it is said, due to this prenatal shock).

After Rizzio's murder, Mary attempted reconciliation with her husband to separate him from his murderous allies, but the reunion quickly dissolved into mutual rancor. Darnley moved out, and Mary found her next infatuation: James Hepburn, a handsome yet desperate adventurer who had recently inherited the earldom of Bothwell. On his advice Mary did the unthinkable. She pardoned Rizzio's murderers, whom Darnley had abandoned and who were seeking revenge. The only explanation for this sudden turn and betrayal of alliances is dynastic. By January 1567, Mary would have known she was pregnant again—this time with Bothwell's baby. To keep the child legitimate in the eyes of her countrymen, she had to stay married to Darnley until the baby was born.

When Darnley took ill in Glasgow, Mary personally brought him back to Edinburgh and lodged him at Kirk O'Field, an isolated mansion outside the city. Nine days later, the house blew up in an enormous explosion. The house was totally demolished, but Darnley was found strangled in the garden. Almost everyone believed that Bothwell and Mary were co-conspirators in the murder. The impetuous couple seemed not to care what people thought, and they married on May 15. This was the beginning of the end for Mary. Now widely regarded as her husband's murderer, and—worse—as a queen who would allow her crush on an adventurer to taint her throne, she was forced to surrender to her half-brother Moray, who now led the nobles against her. She was led a prisoner into Edinburgh amid cries of "Burn the whore!" and imprisoned in Loch Leven castle. True to form, she charmed her jailer's grandson into helping her escape in 1568, but not before miscarrying Bothwell's twins and abdicating the throne to her son, James. She then fled to England, where she lived in captivity until—by her cousin Elizabeth's command—she was escorted to the scaffold in 1587.

▶ Remember: Mary proved herself a talented monarch, but was undone by self-indulgence. She allowed her weaknesses to rule her rather than her many strengths. Strengths and weaknesses are like muscles: they develop only if they are exercised. Be tough on yourself.

Why Croesus Wasn't Happy

Value money for what it can do, not as an end in itself

Michael Romanov was connected to the deposed tsarist family of Russia. When he arrived penniless in America, he entered the restaurant business and built a considerable fortune. A patron once asked him how it felt now that he was a success. "I was a success when I was sleeping on a park bench," replied Romanov coldly. "The only difference is one of comfort."

A Greek myth tells us Bacchus, the god of wine, was so impressed by the lavish hospitality of Midas, the king of Phyrgia, that he offered in return to grant the king whatever wish he wanted. Midas asked that everything he touched be turned to gold. The wish was granted, but Midas was horrified to discover that everything he touched *did* turn to gold, including his daughter and his food.

The myth—with its lesson about greed—was as well known twenty-five centuries ago as it is today, but one man in particular should have paid more attention to it.

"Rich as creosote," Huck Finn said, and Tom Sawyer corrected him, "Rich as Croesus, you mean." The man whose name became synonymous with extraordinary wealth was an actual king, the fifth of his line to rule Lydia in Asia Minor. During his reign the kingdom became rich from trade between Asia and Greece. Croesus gained his reputation for great wealth not only from his generous donations of gold and silver to the Temple at Delphi and the Temple of Artemis at Ephesus (one of the seven wonders of the world), but also from the fact that he began the first official coinage of money.

Herodotus, the "father of history," relates the story of his downfall. If it isn't one of the first lessons of history, at least it is a lesson from one of the first historians.

The famed Athenian lawgiver Solon came to visit Croesus at the height of his reign. Solon was on a ten-year sabbatical from Athens, which he left so the Athenians could not change any of his new laws, the first of which being that no laws could be changed without the approval of Solon.

Croesus was eager to impress his famous visitor and spared no effort in displaying all the magnificent treasures of his land. Finally, on the last night of the tour, he held a sumptuous banquet, and nearly bursting with self-admiration, asked Solon of all the men he had seen in his life and on his extensive travels, who was the most happy?

Without blinking, the wise Solon replied, "Tellius of Athens."

Astonished, the king demanded to know why Tellius was the happiest.

Quite simple, replied Solon. While Tellius ruled, his country was prosperous and his people content; he lived to see his children and then his children's children grow into good citizens; and near the end of his life when his countrymen were besieged by an enemy, even at his great age, he rushed into the battle, routed the foe, and died a hero's death on the field of honor.

Somewhat mollified that so good a life would rank first among the happy, Croesus asked who was the second happiest man, expecting that at the minimum he would be given second place. "Cleobis and Bito," Solon answered without hesitation.

The angry king demanded to know why two plebeians were to be considered such happy men.

Because, Solon explained, not only did the two brothers excel at every competition in the Olympic games, but when their mother was to be honored at a festival for Hera in Argos and the oxen could not be found to pull the cart to carry her, they hitched themselves to it and dragged it the inhuman distance of five and forty furlongs, collapsing and dying as they brought it to rest before the temple. The multitudes at the festival were amazed by their feat, and the council ordered two statues to be erected at the Delphic temple in their memory, for by their deaths they gave honor to the mother who had given them life, and so they must be considered among the happiest of men.

Exasperated, Croesus then demanded to know who was the third happiest man Solon had ever known.

Seeing that the king was too full of himself to have learned a thing from what he had told him, Solon then answered, "Count no man happy until he is dead." He explained that life is too full of accident, too easily blown one way and then another by fate, to count any man happy until nothing more could be added or subtracted from one's knowledge of him.

This reply earned Solon no credit with the king, who promptly decided the famous Athenian was a fool for not recognizing Croesus' good fortune. The king sent him on his way.

Herodotus reports, "After Solon had gone away, a dreadful

vengeance, sent of God, came upon Croesus, to punish him, it seems likely, for deeming himself the happiest of men."

This dreadful vengeance was named Cyrus the Great, emperor of Persia.

In 546 B.C. Croesus—as always, full of self-confidence—launched a war against Persia. Cyrus reacted with the decisiveness and speed for which he became famous. He routed the Lydian army, destroyed the capital at Sardis, and took Croesus himself prisoner. As he was about to be burned at the stake, the deposed king remembered Solon's words, and decried his own blindness in not recognizing the true worth of things. Cyrus apparently took pity on him, ordered the fire extinguished, and allowed Croesus to live as a servant in his household.

▶ Remember: Solon gave examples of nobility and sacrifice to describe happiness, which the wealth-obsessed Croesus could not understand. Money is at best a means to an end—and at the least, as oilman H. L. Hunt put it, "a good way to keep score"—but it is not the end itself.

The Pigling on the Wall

Remember where you came from

Call it "Master of the Universe" syndrome: "Since I'm so rich, I must be smart." The logic of it does have a certain seductive appeal, but avoid it, avoid it, and then slip behind the building at the corner and into the alley, turn right, then left, and keep going until you avoid it again. And then look back because it may be gaining on you.

When Samuel Goldwyn arrived in the United States with an unpronounceable Polish surname, he first reduced the long string of syllables to Goldfish. When he and his partner established one of the first studios in Hollywood, they combined the first and last syllables of their names to call the studio Goldwyn. After his partner's death, Goldfish decided he liked the ring of the studio's name more than his own, so he changed his to match its. Someone with the same name sued over Goldwyn's right to use a name he himself had made famous. On hearing the case the judge ruled, "A self-made man has the right to a self-made name."

Reinventing oneself—and renaming oneself—is not an entirely American phenomenon. Diocles, the son of a Dalmatian slave, became after an army coup Gaius Aurelius Valerius Diocletianus Jovius, emperor of the Roman Empire. Diocletian upgraded not only his name but the entire imperial court to a splendor even Caesar Augustus would have coughed at, with pearl-set diadems, jewel-studded robes, and etiquette-enforcing eunuchs.

Similarly, the famous Madame du Barry, mistress to Louis XV, began life as Jeanne Bécu, the daughter of a seamstress. Her astonishing beauty attracted a flock of new male customers to the Parisian millinery shop where she worked as a salesgirl until she was picked up by Jean du Barry, a gambler and procurer for his aristocratic pals. Convinced that in sweet Jeanne he had a "morsel for the king," he led her on strolls through the public gardens at Versailles until at last she caught the king's eye. The king, of course, couldn't commence a dalliance with a mere commoner, so the young girl was quickly married to du Barry's brother, a count, which made her a comtesse. The new husband then retired to his country estates, and the new noblewoman was installed at Versailles.

To give credit where credit is due, Madame du Barry was by all accounts witty and accomplished as well as beautiful. To relate only one story, at her insistence after a particularly fine meal the king awarded its cook the greatest tribute the kings of France could bestow, the blue ribbon of the Grand Cross of the Order of the Holy Spirit. The king had just established a national tradition: informally known by its blue ribbon, *cordon bleu*, this became the highest honor a chef could attain. But the real surprise was that the king had given the first award to a woman—for du Barry had enlisted a female chef to prepare the dinner after the king had made the mistake of remarking that women could not cook.

Like many who have risen from lowly beginnings to high estate, Madame du Barry later had reason to regret her acquired nobility. When the French Revolution came she was guillotined.

Newly acquired wealth, like newly acquired titles, can cause its own set of problems. *Nouveau riche* is a phrase of derision even among people who will never be *riche* themselves. The newly blessed are often—well, let's be more accurate—*usually* tempted to revel in the bounty bestowed on them, flaunting it everywhere they can. And who can blame them? Good fortune is cause for celebration. Then again, today's windfall might be erased by to-morrow's downfall. It pays to remember who you are and where you came from, and not be tempted to flaunt today what you may not have tomorrow.

A charming story about one man's struggle with this lesson appeared in 1244 in the Scottish *Lanercost Chronicle*. The article purported to be the true story of "a man of substance and worthy memory" who was a member of the high bourgeoisie of Paris, Eu-rope's largest city in the thirteenth century and one of its richest. Let's let the unnamed author speak for himself:

> There lived in Norfolk a simple countryman who had many children, among whom he specially loved a little boy named William, for whom he set aside a pigling and the profits thereof, in order that, grown to manhood, he might provide for himself with-out burdening his parents, wheresoever Fortune might favor him.
>
> The boy followed his father's bidding; and, leaving his father-land, he hastened to France with naught else in his purse but the profits of that pig; for at home his playfellows were wont to call him the Boy of the Pigling.
>
> Now it came to pass, among the miseries and evils of those folk [*the image of a Parisians has not much changed among English-speaking writers*], he so advanced himself as to espouse an honorable matron, the widow of a man of some substance; with whom he had wealth and honor and a household of servants. This he did; and being a

man of diligence in all his works he profited much, and was often-times summoned to business conferences by the king and his great men. From henceforward, even as this honest man grew in sub-stance, so did the fickle favor of the people grow with him; and, lest he should find his prosperity as false and perilous as adversity, he caused a most comely chamber to be built and painted within ac-cording to his own choice; whereof he committed the key to none save unto his own care, nor suffered any other, not even his wife, to enter therein. It was his wont, whensoever he returned from the courts of the great, forthwith to neglect all other business and enter into this secret chamber, wherein he would stay as long as he de-sired, and return in melancholy mood to his family.

In process of time, as this custom became inveterate, all were amazed and agape to know what this might mean that they saw; wherefore, having taken counsel, they called all his friends together to solicit this wise man for the reason of his so strange behavior in this chamber.

At last, besieged and importuned by their complaints, he un-locked the door and called them all together to see his secret, the monument of his poverty thus set forth. Amid other ornaments of this chamber, he had caused a pigling to be painted and a little boy holding him by the string; above whose heads was written, in the English tongue:

Wille Gris, Wille Gris, Thinche cwat you was, and qwat you es!

[Willy Gris, Willy Gris, Think what you was, and what you is!]

▶ **Remember: Don't fool yourself into believing that your good for-tune resulted solely from your own brilliance. Like Willy Gris, you were given a start, a chance, or a lift—maybe you were even given a pigling. Remember your roots.**

The Case of the King's Stolen Fringes

Stay calm

When Sir Francis Drake was playing bowls on Plymouth Hoe in 1588, a messenger dashed up to the grounds with the news that the Spanish Armada was approaching. Not to be interrupted, Drake looked around at his fellow officers and said, "First, we'll finish the game and then we'll beat the Spaniards." His officers, aflame at the news of imminent invasion, calmed down and continued bowling. Drake, of course, beat the Spaniards, although it is not recorded who won the game.

In one of his first commands, the Duke of Wellington was leading a campaign against the Hindu states of central India. In the early morning before a major battle, he rode out with an aide to check the position of the opposing forces. The air was heavy with mist, and the aide was slow to realize, with horror, that they were galloping into the enemy's camp. "By God, sir!" he shouted. "We are in the enemy lines!" Wellington calmly turned his horse's head and, mimicking his aide's language, quietly replied, "By God, sir, so we are." The pair then carefully retraced their steps before the astonished enemy had the presence of mind to kill them.

Another example of English aplomb comes from the eye-witness account of a ship's surgeon in World War II: "I saw the Captain of a ship drinking a cup of tea on the bridge in the course of a dive-bombing attack. While he was drinking the look-out reported, 'Aircraft on the starboard bow, sir.' He did not even look up. At 'Aircraft diving, sir,' the Captain only glanced up. 'Bomb released, sir,' and the Captain gave the order, 'Hard a-starboard,' and went on drinking his tea until the bomb hit the water nearby. The reaction to this episode was a kind of schoolboy hero-worship on the part of everyone who saw it. When the bombing had ceased, the Captain went down to his cabin and when he was alone he wept."

The French term for this admirable composure is *sang-froid* (literally, "cold blood"), and the French no doubt feel they have a patent on it. In 1962 terrorists fired on Charles de Gaulle's car in the outskirts of Paris. Shots punctured the tires and blew out the back window. As the car swerved wildly a bodyguard yelled at de Gaulle and his wife to duck, but neither flinched. When the car finally stopped, de Gaulle got out, brushing shattered glass off his clothing, and remarked, "They really are bad shots."

President de Gaulle's *sang-froid* is a characteristic the French expect in their leaders, and none exemplified it so well (and at times so humorously) as King Louis XIV.

This particular King Louis mastered the art of composure at a very young age. When he was ten years old, a Parisian mob stormed the royal palace and broke into his bedroom. But when the crowd saw their prince sitting calmly on his bed and looking at them without fear, they stopped in their tracks. Thinking better of the trespass, they then turned and fled. The incident appears to have taught young Louis a valuable lesson. He would maintain a calm, collected manner for the rest of his life, even when dealing with national crises, political intrigue, and the human foibles that were his daily diet at seventeenth-century Versailles.

Louis' reign was veritable palace theater that featured tragedy and a few doses of comedy. When he made the dangerous decision to place his grandson on the Spanish throne, he became involved in the inextricable War of the Spanish Succession, and the Austrian Hapsburgs, Holland, and Great Britain were pitted against him. Prince Eugene and the Duke of Marlborough administered defeat after crushing defeat to a France that was drained of men and money, beset by famine and disease, and driven to its lowest depths in international prestige. The king even watched his own son and grandson die. Yet he maintained his dignity through it all, amazing those who surrounded him and strengthening his subjects' morale.

The most telling anecdote about Louis XIV is the Case of the Stolen Fringes. In July 1694, a thief broke into the palace and snipped off the crimson velvet hangings in the Grand Gallery—an extraordinary event since the room was full of people during the daytime, closed and locked at night, and guarded around the clock. This brazen theft caused an outcry. The king was exceedingly displeased, but his faithful valet and attendant, Alexandre Bontems, failed to discover any leads.

A few days later, the king and his family were sitting at the supper table with a crowd of courtiers pressing from behind (the royal dinner, like everything else, being a public event) and Saint-Simon, the royal biographer, enjoying a full view of the guests. Suddenly, a large black object sailed through the air and landed with a shattering crash at the king's end of the table. Louis did not bat an eyelid. He turned to see what had been deposited in front of him and said with a sigh, "This must be my missing fringes."

Saint-Simon describes the bundle as wider than a priest's hat, two feet tall, and shaped like a pyramid. It had sailed through the doorway that separated the dining room from the antechamber, and in midair a piece of fringe had fallen out and landed in the king's wig. Livry, a gentleman-in-waiting, tactfully plucked it out. Livry then reached for the bundle that sat on the table like a modernist centerpiece and opened it. The king was right. It contained the missing fringes along with a note. Louis stretched out his hand, saying, "Let me see," but Livry passed it to the royal physician instead. Saint-Simon peeped over the doctor's shoulders and noticed that the handwriting was a woman's. It read, "Take back your fringes, Bontems. They are not worth the trouble of keeping. My compliments to the King!"

"Well," said the king, unshaken, "that is very insolent. Remove it at once." He did not say another word. Dinner continued as if nothing had happened.

No one thought to close the door after the incident, and no one checked the other rooms for intruders until forty-five minutes later, after the king had finally risen from the table and impassively left the room. The thief who had stolen the fringes and returned them in so bold a manner was never found. Louis' reputation for *sang-froid* entered into legend.

▶ Remember: Great storms, and even little gales, call for steadiness. While not many of us can remain as composed as Louis, discipline yourself to keep calm and in control. You will impress those around you, and you may even find that a little wind now and then clears the air.

Why Leif Ericsson Ignored America

Put personal feelings aside

Like father, like son? Don't bet on it.

The surprise is not that Leif Ericsson discovered America five hundred years before Columbus. After all, the distance from Greenland to America is only half the distance of Iceland to Greenland, or Norway to Iceland—and the sturdy Viking seamen had no problem hopping from Norway to Iceland to Greenland. America was the easiest of their discoveries.

The surprise is that Leif Ericsson's Vikings didn't settle America and claim it for their own. That's what they did with every new other territory they found, whether inhabited or not. England put up a fierce resistance, but the Vikings established their Danelaw over half the island. The Irish tribes resisted as well, but the Vikings made Dublin into their own city and held it for two hundred years. America would have been the greatest and richest settlement of all. Yet Ericsson deliberately refused to colonize it.

What held Ericsson back? If character is destiny, as some like to say, nothing we know of him indicates he was anything but a Viking through and through. The Norse sagas describe him as "big and strong" with a "striking appearance" and "shrewd." But the sagas give us a hint when they also describe him as "in every respect a temperate, fair-dealing man."

Nobody would have ever said that about Leif's father, Eric the Red.

Eric the Red was a rogue, an adventurer, a liar, and a murderer—and only because of his crimes did the Vikings discover Greenland. Exiled from Norway for manslaughter, he went to join the Viking colonies on Iceland. Immediately he got into some sort of scuffle in which a colonist was killed, and so was packed off to a remote village on the opposite coast. True to form, in no time at all he was involved in another fracas, with the by-now predictable killing, and this time the Viking council was in no mood to tolerate him. In 982 he was ordered off the island.

Eric had now earned the sobriquet by which he would be known to history—the Red. The name had nothing to do with his hair—plenty of Norsemen had red hair—but with the blood that flowed whenever he was near.

Eric was not without his charms, and since he had no choice, he convinced some ne'er-do-well friends to join him in a great adventure. They built Viking ships and set sail to the west, where an island had supposedly been sighted by some storm-tossed Norsemen a half-century before.

Only five hundred miles to the west, land was spotted. A vast subcontinent reared up before Eric's eyes, and as he sailed inland he discovered fjords and meadows like those of his native Norway. With his small band, he constructed some dwellings and soon a wonderful idea struck him. His banishment from Iceland was only for three years. With the natural penchant of the Norse to keep moving, he could do pretty well by himself with this property. So he began laying out sites for homes and setting boundaries for farmland. By the time his banishment was over, Eric the Red—now Eric the Real Estate Promoter—was ready.

He named the island Greenland. Of course, it was mostly ice. Ironically Iceland—from which he had been banished—was mostly green.

The promotion was a success. His first sales trip to Iceland brought more than four hundred immigrants, with more to follow. Fairly soon Eric had his own little kingdom, informal to be sure, but far from the reach of Viking councils.

The only problem was the grueling wind, sleet, and unending snow. From high in the mountains above their little settlement, the Greenlanders could see out on the horizon the suggestions of yet another land mass to the west.

Contracting the usual wanderlust, and perhaps hoping that another Iceland, with its more moderate climate and inviting terrain, might lie not far beyond, Eric's son, Leif, decided to take a look. In 1001 he set out with thirty-five men. Eric had wanted to go, but when his horse stumbled on the way down to the ships, he concluded that it was a bad omen and bid his son to sail without him.

Leif and his crew did not have to travel far before spotting Baffin Island. Sailing southeast, they next saw the thickly forested countryside of Labrador. Farther southward they came to a pleasant landing spot in what is now known as Newfoundland. Leif named the place Vinland, and found it so pleasant that he decided to stay over for the winter. The days were longer than in Greenland, the winters much milder, the meadows rich with such grass that their cattle wouldn't need fodder, and the rivers packed with salmon.

On his return to Greenland the following spring, he probably intended to do just what his father had done in Greenland, that is, round up some settlers and head back to the new land. But his father's death shortly after the discovery made him ruler of Greenland. Another voyage was impractical at the moment, so he sent his sister instead.

This second expedition was notable for the Vikings' first encounter with the natives. They were friendly enough at the start, but when the Vikings started acting more like settlers than visitors, the natives attacked. The heroine of the battle was Leif's sister, Freydis "the Fearless." When the Vikings fled from the sudden onslaught, Freydis' pregnancy slowed her down, so she snatched up the sword of a dead Viking, turned on the natives, bared her breasts, and made such terrible noises that they stopped in their tracks and retreated. The Vikings then quickly made for their ships and set sail for Greenland.

Freydis was set on returning to Vinland. She organized another expedition of several ships. When one of the ships arrived before her own, two brothers picked out the original stone building built by Leif years before as a good place for their families. But Freydis was the daughter of Eric the Red. When she discovered

Barker, John W. *Justinian and the Later Roman Empire*. Madison, Wis.: University of Wisconsin Press, 1966.

Barzini, Luigi. *The Italians*. New York: Atheneum, 1983.

Bates, David. *William the Conqueror*. London: Philip, 1989.

Boorstin, Daniel J. *The Americans: The Democratic Experience*. New York: Vintage, 1974.

————. *The Discoverers*. New York: Random House, 1983.

Bosworth, C. E. *The Ghaznavids*. Edinburgh: Edinburgh University Press, 1963.

Browne, E. G. *Chahar Maqala (The Four Discourses) of Samarqandi*. London: E. J. W. Gibb Memorial Trust, 1921.

Browning, Robert. *Justinian and Theodora*. London: Thames & Hudson, 1987.

Bur, Michel. *Suger: Abbé de Saint-Denis Régent de France*. Paris: Perrin, 1991.

Butler's Lives of the Saints. Edited by Herbert J. Thurston and Donald Attwater. Westminster, Md.: Christian Classics, 1987.

Catherine of Siena—Passion for the Truth, Compassion for Humanity: Selected Spiritual Writings. Edited by Mary O'Driscoll. New Rochelle, N.Y.: New City Press, 1993.

Catholic Encyclopedia. Electronic copyright 1996 by New Advent Inc. (Web site).

Chernow, Ron. *The House of Morgan*. New York: Atlantic Monthly Press, 1990.

Chesterton, G. K. *St. Thomas Aquinas*. Garden City, N.Y.: Doubleday, 1956.

Clark, Kenneth. *Civilisation: A Personal View*. New York: Harper & Row, 1969.

Copleston, Frederick C. *Aquinas*. Baltimore: Penguin, 1967.

Cordingly, David. *Under the Black Flag: The Romance and the Reality of Life Among the Pirates*. New York: Random House, 1995.

The Correspondence of Gregory VII: Selected Letters from the Registrum. Translated and with an Introduction by Ephraim Emerton. Columbia Records of Civilization Series. New York: Columbia University Press, 1990.

Crosby, Sumner McKnight. *The Royal Abbey of Saint-Denis: From*

Bibliography

Adams, Jeremy duQuesnay. *Patterns of Medieval Society*. Engle-
wood Cliffs, N.J.: Prentice-Hall, 1969.

Adamson, J. H., and H. F. Foll. *The Shepherd of the Ocean*. Boston:
Gambit, 1969.

The Alexiad of Anna Comnena. Translated by E. R. A. Sewter. Baltimore: Penguin, 1969.

Arberry, A. J. *Classical Persian Literature*. London: George Allen
and Unwin, 1958.

Asser, John. *Alfred the Great: Asser's Life of King Alfred and Other
Contemporary Sources*. Translated and with an Introduction
by Simon Keynes and Michael Lapidge. New York: Penguin,
1983.

Athanasius. *The Life of Antony and the Letter to Marcellinus*. Translated and with an Introduction by Robert C. Gregg. New York:
Paulist Press, 1980.

Aubrey, John. *Brief Lives*. Edited by O. L. Dick. London: Secker
and Warburg, 1949.

the brothers' effrontery, she had them thrown out of the house and killed. She wanted their families killed, too. When her men refused to go that far, she personally waded in with an ax to slaughter the brothers' women and children.

On the return to Greenland, Freydis' story was that the brothers had decided to stay behind. But sailors talk, and soon Leif got wind there was something more to the story. He tortured three of Freydis' men until the truth was exposed. Leif's own sister had murdered families the Viking chief was honor-bound to protect. Enraged as he was by this challenge to his authority, the chieftain could not bring himself to kill or banish Freydis, but in history's eye he did something of greater consequence. He laid a Viking curse on her and her progeny—and, it seems, on Vinland itself. No Viking ever dared to make the voyage again.

The Vikings left behind so little on American soil that historians would have trouble believing they set foot there until twentieth-century archaeologists uncovered traces of their presence.

A rich new world, far more bounteous than any the Vikings had ever known, was surrendered, even proscribed, with its memory only dimly kept alive in half-remembered sagas, because the son of Eric the Red would have nothing to do with blood.

▶ Remember: Leif was diverted from his goal by his rage. Vinland presented the greatest opportunity in the long history of Viking colonization, but Leif let an affront to his code color his judgment. Eventually harsh Greenland was abandoned by his descendents, while bountiful America awaited Columbus.

Scullen, Howard H. *Scipio Africanus: Soldier and Politician.* London: Thames & Hudson, 1970.

Shafritz, Jay M. *Words on War: Military Quotations from Ancient Times to the Present.* New York: Simon & Schuster, 1990.

Shenkman, Richard. *Legends, Lies and Cherished Myths of American History.* New York: William Morrow, 1988.

Shenkman, Richard, and Kurt Reiger. *One-Night Stands with American History.* New York: William Morrow, 1980.

Smith, Philip J. *Scipio Africanus and Rome's Invasion of Africa: A Commentary on Titus Livius, Book xxix.* Amsterdam: Gielen, 1993.

Smyth, William. *The Lessons of History.* New York: Simon & Schuster, 1955.

Sola Pool, Ithiel de. *Candidates, Issues, and Strategies: Computer Simulation in the 1960 Election.* Cambridge, Mass.: MIT Press, 1964.

Stein, Aurel. *Ancient Khotan.* 2 vols. Oxford: Oxford University Press, 1907.

Stenton, F. M. *Anglo-Saxon England.* Oxford: Clarendon Press, 1971.

Stepto, M. *The Lieutenant Nun: Memoir of a Basque Transvestite in the New World.* Boston: Beacon Press, 1996.

Sun-tzu. *The Art of War.* New York: Delacorte Press, 1983.

Tierney, Brian. *The Crisis of Church and State, 1050–1300.* Toronto: University of Toronto Press in association with the Medieval Academy of America, 1988.

Tolstoy, Leo. *War and Peace.* New York: Random House, 1992.

Train, John T. *Famous Financial Fiascos.* New York: Clarkson Potter, 1985.

Troyat, Henri. *Alexander of Russia.* New York: Fromm International, 1986.

Ullmann, Walter. *The Papacy and Political Ideas in the Middle Ages.* London: Variorum Reprints, 1976.

Weisheipl, James A. *Friar Thomas D'Aquino: His Life, Thoughts, and Work.* Garden City, N.Y.: Doubleday, 1974.

White, Theodore H. *In Search of History.* New York: Harper & Row, 1978.

Williamson, Trevor. "Pox: 200 Years of Vaccination." University of the West of England, 1996 (Web site).

Wofford, Suzanne L. *The Choice of Achilles: The Ideology of Figure in the Epic.* Palo Alto, Calif.: Stanford University Press, 1992.

Wriggins, Sally H. *Xuanzang: A Buddhist Pilgrim on the Silk Road.* Boulder, Colo.: Westview, 1996.

Zanker, Graham. *The Heart of Achilles: Characterization of Personal Ethics in The Iliad.* Ann Arbor: University of Michigan Press, 1994.